LOOKING FOR EAGLES

LOOKING

FOR

EAGLES

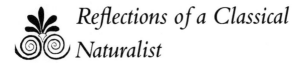

Reflections of a Classical Naturalist

JANET LEMBKE

 LYONS & BURFORD, PUBLISHERS

Printed in the United States of America

10 9 8 7 6 5 4 3 2 1

Permission from the following to quote copyrighted material is gratefully acknowledged:

The Johns Hopkins University Press: ten-line excerpt, "Hymn to Artemis," from *Callimachus: Hymns, Epigrams, Select Fragments* edited and translated by Stanley Lombardo and Diane Rayor, © 1988 by The Johns Hopkins University Press.

Macmillan Publishing Company: Lines from "Leda and the Swan" are reprinted with permission of Macmillan Publishing Company from *The Poems of W.B. Yeats: A New Edition,* edited by Richard J. Finneran. Copyright 1928 by Macmillan Publishing Company, renewed 1956 by Georgie Yeats.

Some of the material, in slightly different form, has appeared or is scheduled to appear in these periodicals:

Bird Watcher's Digest, forthcoming: "The Swan That Fathered the Trojan War" and "The Children of Picus"
The North American Review, Vol. 274, No. 1 (March 1989): "Looking for Eagles"
Sierra, Vol. 73, No. 4 (July/August 1988): "The Menhaden's Nursemaid"

Library of Congress Cataloging-in-Publication Data

Lembke. Janet.
    Looking for eagles : reflections of a classical naturalist / Janet Lembke.
        p.   cm.
    ISBN 1-55821-077-6 :$19.95
    1. Nature. 2. Natural history—Outdoor books. I. Title.
QH81.L54 1990
508—dc20   90-41041
                                                                  CIP

for Sarah, my mother,
and in memory of my father, Joseph

Contents

‹‹‹-‹‹‹-‹‹‹-‹‹‹-‹‹‹-‹‹‹-‹‹‹-‹‹‹-‹‹‹-‹‹‹-‹‹‹-‹‹‹-‹‹‹-‹‹‹-‹‹‹-‹‹‹-‹‹‹-‹‹‹-

Acknowledgments

Many of the people at Great Neck Point who helped me find these stories are mentioned here by name. Others farther afield also came to my aid:

Joseph Bruchac, who searched for ticks in the underbrush of Indian legends—but found none

Robert Fagles, who discovered, in a sea of Greek, the most joyfully numinous English names for the Nereids

Allen Hale, who knows his nightingales even when their nomenclature undergoes transformation

John Herington, who gave breath to the portrayal of D'Arcy Wentworth Thompson

Stanley Lombardo and Diane Rayor, who rendered Kallimakhos' "Hymn to Artemis" into English that can be smelled, touched, and tasted, as well as seen and heard

Sara Mack, who pointed out Picus' exact location in the dense leaves of Ovid

Thanks go winging to you all and to Peter Burford, who kept these tales from turning into wind-eggs.

Introduction

C lassical naturalist—what's *that*?" Someone following devoutly in the giant footsteps of Thoreau, John Muir, Henry Best, and Aldo Leopold? No. My mentors are Aristotle, Pliny, and a few ancient poets. Let me explain.

I live at the confluence of two broad streams. One is wet, salty, and huge: the lower Neuse, more southerly of the two muscular rivers that pour into North Carolina's Pamlico Sound. The second runs invisible but hardly silent, though ears cease to hear it as they cease to hear traffic or the ticking of a clock. It's the Greco-Roman tributary that flows with steady, unobtrusive force through Western languages and culture.

There are reasons, of course, for standing at such an unlikely junction. One is that when I married a retired chief petty officer, both of us past the half-century mark, I also married his home—his burrow—on the banks of the Neuse. The other reason is that the Greco-

1

Roman tributary has surged through imagination as long as I can remember. I was born to it and dunked in it repeatedly by family and education. A degree in Classics has led to twenty-plus years of time-travel to the Rome and Athens of the centuries B.C. There I've poked into and under old poems and plays (an exercise something like turning over old logs to see what wiggles beneath the decaying wood). Back home in the present, I try to find English equivalents that do not stupefy a contemporary audience but recreate the excitement that earned not only acclaim and prizes for the ancient originals but millennia of survival. And in some cockeyed, vital way, as the Chief pulls fish from our net or I prowl the shore, dog trotting along, to compile nest-records for the area's birds or we sit in the yard simply watching the river, long immersion in the classical past enhances understanding of the present riparian moment and its abounding wildlife.

The here-and-now scene for the stories is this: the river and a rural community ignored by road maps but identified on the nautical chart for the lower Neuse as Great Neck Point, an isolated peninsula inhabited and cherished by people almost as wild as the landscape. A thousand years ago, Indians saw much the same maritime forest that meets our eyes—sweet gums, pines decked in untidy swags of greenbriar and trumpet vine, live oaks and baldy cypress bearded with grey Spanish moss, stands of yaupon holly, wax myrtles, and palmettoes. They saw the mixed woods inland— maples, deciduous oaks, hickories, and hackberries

2

amid the conifers. Fields interrupt the woods today and bear crops of corn, soybeans, cabbages, or waist-high weeds. Throughout the peninsula, creeks meander as they always have, guarded by needlerushes and giant cordgrass.

Richness of habitat and our location at a temperate latitude hospitable to both northern and southern species afford shelter to more critters than could crowd aboard an ark. Brown pelicans perched on pilings and towhees calling from hedgerows find equal welcome. White-tailed deer browse at the edges of the soyfields; black bear ramble in the deep woods. Migrating monarch butterflies mingle in season with the ubiquitous swallowtails. Black-and-yellow argiope spiders weave blatant webs while black widows lurk in cinderblocks. Bluefish, blue crabs, shrimp, and carp, cooter turtles and cottonmouths share the river with otters and dolphins.

So far, the Point's human population has not competed seriously with the wildlife for living space. Creatures have flourished because they've been left alone, with *anthropos* kept in check by the timber companies that own much of the peninsula's acreage and have planted it with vast tracts of loblolly pines. For generations, these pines have stood like palisades against urban encroachments. People who have found their way to the Point also flourish because they, too, have been left alone. Wild animals and wild people, however, may all be threatened species now that timber companies have discovered more money in developing waterfront lots than in growing trees.

3

Meanwhile, isolation works its wonders. Lack of urban services fosters a frontier spirit and impels Great Neck Pointers to cantankerous self-reliance. And isolation connects us intimately with sun, wind, earth, and water. The river-world provides our clocks and calendars. The Chief and I are rarely sure of the date, but we know the season and the hour of day. Spanish mackerel are running, crabpots fill overnight, sea nettles sting unwary swimmers: midsummer. Striped mullet bulge with roe, canvasbacks and black scoter begin to raft, migrating veeries feast on tupelo berries: October. Lion's mane jellyfish bob on the waves, and yellow-rumped warblers chip in the hedgerows: winter. Returning orchard orioles bugle brisk chow-calls and bobolinks, passing through, sing rinky-tink tunes from greening mimosas: late April, the river is warm enough to wade—high time that fish nets were repaired; time, too, that tomatoes, squash, bell peppers, and speckled butterbeans were planted. Sun, moon, and stars, and our internal rounds of hunger and sleep infallibly tell us the hour. We set ourselves to their cycles, to the seasons turning like a moving wheel, and to the ever-insistent water.

Animals and people—the river flows benign or storms like a stampede through all we do and are. What we see at this point in its course is the widest of all the country's wide rivers: here, the Neuse stretches five miles shore to shore. For most of its upstream reaches, it's hardly more than a brook. At New Bern, a town that's a recent hiccup in the river's long history, the Neuse gathers force in its easterly thrust, rolls ever

4

wider toward the Sound, and bends ninety degrees to the north just before it flows past Great Neck Point. At the Rounding, as oldtimers call the bend, the water becomes saline, home to shrimp and oysters and ocean-going fish. The saltiness, however, and the river's rise and fall have little to do with astronomical tides, for Pamlico Sound lies twelve miles distant, too far down-river for the moon's tug to affect the level of the water here. The salt and salt-loving creatures arrive from the Sound on random northerly winds, and a steady blow from that quarter can cause the river to rise a foot in mere minutes, can keep it pummeling the undersides of piers for days on end. The river falls and stays low when winds drive out of the south.

High or low, calm or rough—and it heaves mighty rough at times—the river has ever been a road, traveled in its depths by marine life, overhead by birds, and on its surface, only a blip of time ago, by human-kind. People may have first set eyes on the Neuse sometime between 8000 and 4000 B.C.; a jasper projectile point manufactured during that archaic period was recently found on the undeveloped shore just up-river from our community. Other, later Indians paddled the river in their log canoes, set up fish camps on its banks, and left behind shards of their clay pots. In 1584, one of Sir Walter Raleigh's explorers sailed his pinnace here and named the river for the band of Indians, the Neusiok, whose fief it was. The upstart colonists arrived in the early 1700s, and for two centuries the river bustled with trade and transport, wooden ships bringing Old-World goods and colonizers to the

New World, vessels freighting the produce of farmers and the catches of fishermen, boats bearing cargoes of naval stores or towing rafts of timber to the mills. Lately, such river traffic has diminished; a few trawlers and commercial crabbers work the water amid a scurry of small recreational craft. Fish and birds, though, ply the river today much as they always have.

When I tug a flapping seatrout from the summer net or glimpse a kittiwake blown upriver from its usual pelagic haunts by a January storm, when I see the replica of the small, stout vessel that led Sir Walter's expedition set her square-rigged sails for the first time and proceed at a full-breasted, matronly pace upriver to New Bern, when I find an Indian potsherd on the sand, how easy it is to slip off today, slide into yesterday, and bob up again for breath in the present. The river is not just a road but an umbilical link between then and now. Here on the river, past and present overlap, mingle, and marry.

The river has surely spawned legends and given rise to whole cosmogenies. There must have been Neusiok versions of *Genesis:* how the earth, its people, plants and animals came to be, how the river itself came to course through this land. Gods must have been named and praised for their gifts and feared for their swift unpredictability. But when the Indians of the lower Neuse were virtually wiped out by war, slavery, and disease, their legends died with them, and the gods fell silent. Only tantalizing scraps remain, preserved as curiosities by European settlers. One tale was hinted at by John Lawson, an eighteenth-century English gentleman who traveled among the Carolina Indians and recorded his copious observations. Much of his reporting is fair and historically valuable, but his snort at the end of one passage is audible today. He mentions hearing "a long Tale of a great Rattle-Snake, which, a great while ago, liv'd by a Creek in that River (which was *Neus*) and that it kill'd abundance of *Indians;* but at last a bald Eagle kill'd it, and they were rid of a Serpent, that us'd to devour whole Canoes full of *Indians,* at a time." Now, the snort: "I have been something tedious on this Subject, on purpose to shew what strange, ridiculous Stories these Wretches are inclinable to believe."

Sounds like a twist on something that might have happened in the Garden of Eden. I wish John Lawson had inquired more deeply into the Snake and the Eagle. I wish I had access to the lost tales and the vanished perceptions of reality to which they gave voice. But, like nature, imagination abhors a vacuum. Lacking the river's original stories, I do what I can, bringing to the void a few ideas and legends and a principle found in the Greco-Roman past. Bubbling up from deep layers, they flow into the riverscape as if their wellsprings were indeed here, not half a world and two millennia away. As surely as wind salts the river with water pushed in from the sea, the classics season my views of all that is immediately available to my senses.

The river-world and antiquity meet in the bookcase as well as in my imagination. Aristotle's *History of Animals,* written in the fourth century B.C., and the later opus of Pliny, the Roman natural historian (and

7

fabulist), sit unabashed on the reference shelves beside Roger Tory Peterson, McClane's *Field Guide to Saltwater Fishes of North America,* and the volumes identifying everything from wildflowers to reptiles and jellyfish. Poets and playwrights rest also in this company—Homer, Pindar and Aeschylus, Euripides, Ovid, along with several American and British poets of the present century. Do I hear a snort? (Poor woman, she's as inclinable a Wretch as any John Lawson met.) What have strange, ridiculous, literary stories to do with natural history? Plenty.

To begin with, Latin and Greek are the languages of scientific nomenclature. Myths lie hidden within the tough shells of binomial taxonomy like seeds waiting for proper sprouting weather. They also shine in the constellations like beacons waiting to be seen and followed. Eagles and osprey, woodpeckers, dolphins, snakes, and spiders—ancient eyes observed and variously interpreted the same natural phenomena that offer themselves to our inspection. Ancient inquisitiveness asked the same questions that recur to our intelligence: What is it? How does it work? Is it good or bad, and *why*? Under modern rationality's cold, fluorescent glare, many of the old answers look as useful as a cast-off wine jug—the paint is still bright, the designs handsome, but the clay is terminally cracked. Come-lately knowledge of scientific facts does not, however, render the antique stories less enchanting, for the myths and legends, suppositions and superstitions document one phase of the human struggle to understand all that presents itself to reason.

I have taken as my chief mentors the Greeks of the early fifth century B.C., a time at which the heady wine of archaic perception had only begun to be watered down with new points of view. The world of Aeschylus and Pindar is a world that has not yet conceived of metaphor. It makes no comparisons. Things are themselves and, at the same time, anything else. If Zeus is said to be a bird, that's precisely what he *is,* not what he's like. Rivers literally give birth to children and armies. The ground of a battlefield is murderous in its own right. Cities put down real roots so that they may tap sustenance from the earth. The leaves of a victor's chaplet are wings at the moment of victory and truly lift him off the ground. Everything human and natural is alive and connected irrevocably to everything else, a concept that may at first seem a direct ancestor of current ecological thinking about the web of life. No, for the Greeks tossed inanimate objects—rocks, water, metals, cities—into the pot along with living organisms. Every visible, tangible piece of reality was understood as the instrument, shelter, or temporal embodiment of unseen, timeless, sacred energies.

The Greeks also espoused a principle by which people might deal with these omnipresent energies, a principle that has not made its way West from the classical world. The Greeks transmitted to us the concept of democracy and the base for our emphasis on the importance of the individual. But we've lost their way of viewing the relationship between humankind and nature and of understanding all nature, organic and inorganic, as alive and sentient. Holy, if you will, because infused with the divine. The Greeks saw people as beings irremediably severed from the divine but able, with care, to live in concert with its manifestations—the flora and fauna in their myriad forms, the constellations, bodies of water, and even the stones. For arrogant, self-centered humanity, the watchword was *kairos*—moderation, balance. We who are time-bound, finite, and mortal should step carefully wherever we go lest we provoke catastrophic retaliation from all that is timeless and immortal. People nowadays look to native Americans to find a model for similar reverence. We could, many of us, look back into our own pasts.

As a classical naturalist, one of my goals is conservation, though not in the word's conventional sense of championing and practicing TLC for natural resources. In these stories, that sense assumes a secondary place. The place is important, yes, and close to paramount because concern for the environment comes easily, informally to anyone who muddles around observing birds and toads and isopods in a river-washed near-wilderness. But I, who am propelled by an amateur's passionate curiosity, leave formal advocacy for conservation as it's usually understood to the more knowledgeable others whose passions are shaped not only by the tangible world but by training in the sciences. I cheer them on and would apply the same advocacy, the same TLC to the ancient stories, archaic perceptions, and the principle of *kairos*.

Such a goal may sound more like that of a conservator than a conservationist. It would be if the aim were to preserve this part of the Greco-Roman heritage behind touch-me-not glass. But the myths and ideas are not hands-off museum pieces, beautifully displayed, exquisitely polished, and lacking any sign of life. They belong more properly in a petting zoo. They're here for pleasure as well as edification. Don't just look. Listen. Sniff, taste, touch. Go ahead and squeeze them. They may provoke thought, but they won't ever bite. Yet, they may be as imperiled as *Charadrius melodus,* the piping plover, in these days of little Latin and not an iota of Greek. Their habitat in this country seems to be the ninth grade—a spring through mythology, a passing (or failing) glance at an English translation of Homer's *Odyssey.* It might not be amiss to add a fourth R—Resources—to the long-reigning trinity of the school curriculum. Not only would the planet's natural resources be covered, but also the infinitely touchable, tastable, pleasing, and fully renewable resources of imagination.

Necessary though it seems, such conservation is not the primary impetus that keeps impaling me on green-briar thorns in mosquito-loud woods and sends me tripping over the river's submerged, barnacle-studded tree stumps. The search for eagles is simply a majestic excuse to explore what the river-world offers. Look for one thing, find another. Birds of many feathers, fish of many flavors, a wriggle of snakes, a stick-tight of ticks—surprises come daily, and so do the blessings, not least of which is being able to set life to natural cycles rather than to the stern commandments of a wind-up clock. But the true quest, the one at the heart of all the stumbles, impalements, and astonished joy, focuses on a particular grail—the recovery of an old perception of *Homo* smarty-pants' place in the larger world. I'm really looking for *kairos*.

Looking for Eagles

About a mile up the rush-lined meanders of Courts Creek, a dead cypress stands above the dark water. Towering over most of the pines and sweet gums, it holds a massive pile of weathered logs in a fork near its top. Bald eagles built this construct that's only now beginning to fall apart. The dates of active use have slipped local memory, but our neighbor Bonnie recalls that, oh, a dozen years ago the Audubon Society's headquarters in New York sent a photographer to film the monumental and deserted eyrie. It's big enough to have hatched a Volkswagen.

The nesting eagles have been absent from the lower Neuse in coastal North Carolina for the past several decades. The story of their endangerment is now familiar. Chlorinated hydrocarbons, for which DDT has become a generic name, were the foundation of a ramshackle series of events like those that occurred in the house that Jack built. This is the seed or the insect

13

that lay in the field that the farmer sprayed with pesticide. This is the white-footed mouse, the Southern toad that ate the poisoned grain or bug. This is the bird that dined on the prey it caught in the field and thus absorbed at third- or fourth-hand the killing chemicals. Raptors that fed on terrestrial animals began to vanish, the peregrine falcon notable among them. The chemicals also washed from the soil into the rivers, where they entered the algae and plankton grazed on by larger aquatic species. And the birds that live by fishing, such as osprey and pelicans and bald eagles, absorbed the poisons as they ate their suppers. The reproductive chemistry of these birds was so altered that many eggs had shells fragile enough to break under the weight of an incubating parent. Some had no shells at all. Generations of eggs never hatched. When cause and effect had been discovered and brought to attention, the use of chlorinated hydrocarbons was banned. A few of the feathered victims did escape the pesticide's ravages, enough to give their populations a slim, slow chance for survival but not always enough to fill the visual and aural silences of the past several decades.

A couple of years ago, my immediate neighbors began reporting that they'd seen bald eagles around— soaring over the river, perched on a tree up the creek, hunched over road-kills on the grassy strips that border the road as it winds through a near-wilderness of pine plantations or mixed woods. We had reason to hope that eagles were returning, even if only as sometime visitors rather than as parents who were moving into our area to give their young 'uns a healthy upbringing in the country. The river and woods certainly offer the requisites for good living—a generous food supply, a habitat largely protected from human incursions. And hope wore feathers. It came directly to the river in the form of exploding colonies of osprey and flights of brown pelicans daily where, two years earlier, only a few pouchbills would be seen all summer. Both species have recovered in extravagant fashion. If they could do so on our small slice of the river, why not bald eagles as well? Reports from inland also encouraged hope: the eagles are seen in increasing numbers—a record ninety-six juveniles in 1987—at Jordan Lake near Raleigh. Jordan Lake is an artificial lake created by damming, a haunt for fishermen and boaters, campers and hikers, but the acres in which the young eagles have chosen to summer have been barred to human recreation.

I wasn't sure, though, that I could believe local rumors. The people who said they'd spotted a bald eagle were the people who tried to help the bird-woman by asking if I'd seen the "bluebird."

"Which one?" I'd say. "Big or little? Blue all over?"

"Kinda small, but blue, I mean really blue."

That eliminated the blue jay, large, raucous, carelessly obvious, and easily identified by any novice. But three other birds of startling, eye-arresting blue inhabit our shore. Year-round the Eastern bluebirds perch on electric wires and flock, calling, from pine to pine. This year a pair drove off house sparrows and the mockingbird aggressively ensconced in a nearby myrtle, and they nested successfully in a long vacant box that had once been nailed to a shady tree but was relo-

15

cated to a pole in an open field of the well-mowed sort that bluebirds prefer. Then, at the end of April, the tiny indigo buntings arrive, and the males, electric blue all over, perch on the topmost twigs of sweet-gum trees to sing the high, sweetly lisping couplets that proclaim their territories. At the same time, the blue grosbeaks return for summering, their rusty wing-patches emphasizing the Delft blue of their bodies. They cling, tails flicking, to the stalks of weeds and high grasses; they scold from the hedgerows and honeysuckle tangles where they build their nests and give their presences away with the metallic *pnk* that is their callnote.

I thank good-hearted friends for pointing out the existence of a "bluebird." They act out of a benevolent urge to help me as I wander through their yards behind my binoculars. But can these nice people who lump all blue-colored birds into one category distinguish an eagle from an osprey? Or a northern harrier? Or a turkey vulture teetering as it soars, dark wings held in a flattened V against a white-blue sky?

One neighbor does know birds—Dorothy, landlady of the box now tenanted by the nesting pair of bluebirds. She doesn't go out of her way as I do to locate birds, but she has a keen eye for the natural events taking place in her yard or along the road on her trips to town. She knows a bald eagle when she sees or hears one, a benefit of having been reared in Colorado, superb eagle country in the pre-DDT days, country that is now being repopulated by the species. When Dorothy spoke of seeing an immature eagle hunkered on the logging access road three miles away, her words had credibility.

Of course, I decided to look for eagles, not really expecting to see one but happy to take whatever the search might bring. The quest began by going up Courts Creek to see the abandoned eyrie.

The late-spring expedition was mounted in two inflatable rafts tied together like tandem-trailers. We waded them into the creek mouth and pushed them across the sandbar at the pond's riverward end. In a tangle of arms and legs, Bonnie, her husband Al, and their daughter K. D. fitted themselves into the snug confines of the lead raft. Al rowed, towing the second raft where I lolled, doing no work but battening on pleasure. My husband the Chief was not so idle; as the expedition's official photographer, he sorted lenses and checked camera settings. And we set off. With a quiet, regular swish, Al's oars dipped and rose, bearing green strands of sago pondweed. The light couldn't have been better, the late afternoon sun westering behind us and casting clear light on all that lay ahead.

I remember the duration of the voyage as measured by the quality of light. It deepened in color as we traveled upcreek and down again. At first transparent, it gathered a golden tint of increasing intensity. When we disembarked hours later, the sun was touching the trees on the far, far shore of the Neuse, and the light gleamed with a soft gold-brown luminescence, almost the color of a brown bat's fur.

And on the journey, as oars clunked steadily, they stirred the faintly fetid scent of the decaying weeds that

17

float in matted rafts on the water. Frogs, bass, and striped mullet jumped and splashed back home, the ripples making little waves that bounced the rafts of weeds. A snapping turtle pulled its head under at our approach. Long-billed marsh wrens burbled their tiny rinky-tink songs, and red-winged blackbirds clung silently to the slender stalks of the needlerushes. Here and there along the creek banks, river otters had made mudslides for their play. K. D. spotted a leftover from hunting season, a duck decoy made of plastic. Of course, her father rowed over so that she could retrieve it; it sits now, a souvenir, on the family's front deck.

The creek narrows gradually, from wide pond to closed-in stream bridged by fallen trees draped with Spanish moss. For the low deadfalls we ducked our heads and looked warily for the cottonmouths that could well be stretched out on the branches waiting for prey. A small lithe snake, no cottonmouth but a brown water snake, swam swiftly upstream through the rushes at water's edge.

We had an escort all the way to the eyrie. Osprey tracked our slow progress and called loudly, incessantly. Their chirping cries sound incongruously sweet for such a large raptor, whose wings can reach a spread of six feet, whose talons can lock on a flounder almost big enough to fill a number three washtub. I've seen them often as they fish the river. They fly darkly out of the creek and send the gulls and terns on the sandbar at creek mouth into silent skyward explosions of flight. The white foreheads of the osprey wheeling and calling above us caught glints of gold from the sunlight. Two, three, five of them flew overhead, the black wrist-patches of their light-colored wings showing bold. *Pandion haliaetus*—Pandion the sea-eagle—is the name with which they have been blessed in scientific terminology.

The first part of the name recalls an ancient and barbaric myth. Once upon a time out of time in Greece, Pandion, king of Athens, had two daughters, Procne and Philomela. He gave Procne as a reward for help in battle to Tereus, king of Daulis. After she had born a son, Itys, Tereus wearied of his perhaps talkative wife. He cut out her tongue, cloistered her, and pretended that she was dead. And he rode off to Athens to claim her sister Philomela as his bride. But there's no stopping a loquacious woman, and Procne found a way to speak. Weaving a tapestry that depicted her fate, she communicated the horrid truth to Philomela. In vengeance, the two sisters killed Itys, boiled him, and served him to his faithless father for dinner. And they fled. Tereus, soon realizing what he had eaten, seized an axe and hunted them down. Terrified by his murderous rage, the sisters prayed that the gods turn them into birds. The gods were attentive. Procne became a songless swallow, ancestress to the barn swallows that twitter as they hunt insects in calligraphic flight over our fields. Philomela became a nightingale whose trill *itu itu* repeats the dead boy's name. Tereus, changed to a hawk, hunts them both to this day. And still no end to the changes. Itys, resurrected, became a pheasant; Pandion was transformed to the osprey that still bears his name.

19

Pandion's descendants cried and soared, keeping close watch on our rafts. The reason for such vigilance became apparent as we rounded the last bend. In every one of the taller pines and cypresses near the eagles' one-time home is a similar but smaller construct. The osprey have built their nests around the eyrie like a village risen around a decaying fortress. Seeing the eyrie, I had the sense that we five human pilgrims had participated in a memorial service at a cenotaph.

Looking for eagles at Great Neck Point is mostly a solitary pursuit. People are occupied with jobs, gardens, and gill nets; the nearest bird club is eighty miles away. But I'm not alone in the woods and fields. Sally Doberman accompanies me. She knows I'm going off to hunt again long before we leave the trailer. She reads the signals perfectly. I reach for my brown bandanna: she wakes from the soundest snooze. I tie the bandanna around my head to keep wind from blowing wayward hair into my eyes: she leaps up and whirls in tight, joyful circles. I put binoculars around my neck and reach for the bird-bag, the over-the-shoulder tote that holds field guide, Navy knife, insect repellent, and plastic bags for collecting feathers and flowers, beetles and turtles: Sal lies spatch-cock, legs stretched behind her, and clacks her teeth impatiently. I pick up the three-legged folding stool with aluminum legs and blue canvas seat and sling it over my shoulder: she runs to the door. And off we go, woman and dog, while the Chief shovels fill-dirt into sinkholes by the bulkhead or builds another set of shelves to hold the burgeoning collection of reference books.

Looking for eagles means going to school. In any weather, yard and hedgerows, woods and fields, the rush-lined creek, the river itself provide classrooms where I slog earthbound in search of wings. I've spent fifty years blocking out most sights and sounds except for those demanding human attention. My eyes are as unfocused as those of a two-week-old puppy, open but perceiving the world as streaking, tumbling blurs of color. My ears have been all too selective, shut tight against barking dogs and distant thunder but imme-diately responsive to the telephone's clamor or the cicada-buzz of an alarm clock. Looking for eagles means trying to tune in on the faintest chirp from a hedgerow or a rustle in the spartina grass at the creek, trying to sense, as well, the footsteps of a lizard or a wren. It means struggling to interpret not just noise but the implications of silence. I could also use the puppy's "remarkable motor," as W. H. Auden termed its nose. My nose and tongue are utterly inefficient, too often failing to catch the sweet or pungent flavors of salt, sun, rain, and earth. Even skin and blood need tutoring so that they might learn to signal changes in wind, humidity, and barometric pressure. A battery of idle neural synapses needs to be connected before I can look for eagles with the five classic senses instead of convoluted intellect.

And that's the second lesson: thinking gets in the way. Otter, hawk, seatrout—each is able to merge finite self entirely with the infinite array of real things surrounding that self, but I'll always be an observer standing on the marshy edge of such perception. Shouldn't it be possible, though, to learn to employ

21

the senses intuitively enough to let the body receive some messages directly from outside stimuli without the intervention of analytic thought? If the river were to grant me three wishes, they would be that my eye be made speedy enough to catch and retain the color flashing at the edge of vision; my ear be tuned to home straight in on the source of the elusive call or splash; my nose be taught to sniff out the tender sharpness of coming storm before the sky clouds over. Like the barely exposed root that trips an unwary walker, overt analysis makes perception stumble and fall. The swift colors wink out instantly, cries and odors vanish, and the evidence delivered by the senses lies sprawled in the pine straw of cerebration.

I borrow Sal's alertness. She is aware of birds, not in the flush-'em, fetch-'em manner of pointers and retrievers, but after the fashion of her kind. Dobermans are classified as working dogs, and they're as specialized as the working breeds that pull sleds or herd cattle and sheep. The Doberman's specialty is to zero in, gently or aggressively, on people. Beneath her ferocious black-and-rust disguise, behind the sharp white teeth that glitter when she grins, Sal is peaceable. The Chief and I comprise her full-time occupation. She supervises our fishing and has learned to hold her breath, dive underwater, and retrieve the carcasses of cleaned fish for eating on the spot or burying as other dogs would bury bones. She gives voice when strangers walk along the bulkhead or drive into the yard; though her ears are uncropped (why crop the ears of a dog not destined for the show ring?), she protects by her mere

22

appearance. And she keeps me company, fretting with soft squeaks when rain drums on the trailer's roof, standing at the door to say "Let's go!" when the rain stops. Some of her interest in birds is innate: they call and move in sudden, attention-commanding ways. Some stems undoubtedly from her observations of my interest. Accompanying me, she has trained herself to notice what I notice. I am, after all, her job.

Our rounds take us eight hundred feet upriver through the woods to the small sandy beach at the mouth of Courts Creek. From there we turn inland along a path, bordered by young prickly pears, that skirts the edge of the pond. This path, a wide one, was constructed several years ago by wheels; several families at the Point indulged themselves in three- and four-wheeled all-terrain vehicles in which they careered at full tilt, like Roman charioteers, through wetlands inaccessible by foot. Most of these joy-riding machines are now in the stable, foundered, hallelujah, by mechanical difficulties. From the prickly-pear path, we head up the fence line. The line cuts straight through young deciduous trees that are packed in some places as tightly as toothpicks. The fence, once electrified, is long gone, existing now only as a few strands of rusted wire still bearing freshly bright-red plastic insulators. The fence line brings Sal and me to the pond road, a pine-dark alley that winds over high grass and wild-flowers and deep, water-filled wheel-ruts. When rain-less days turn other puddles into dust, these shadowed pools retain enough moisture for bathing birds and wriggling tadpoles. At the pond, the few fishermen

23

who use the road launch their boats through a gap in the cordgrass. Last year, a found-pier was built at the launching point—found because its pilings and decking were salvaged after a severe nor'easter had dismantled other piers and blown their lumber up the creek and into the pond. From the pier, Sal and I retrace our steps along the pond road and arrive at the dirt right-of-way that gives the residents in our section of the Point access to their homes. I mosey in a downriver direction along the dirt road while Sal runs through fallow fields and roots in the hedgerows on either side. Three-tenths of a mile farther, we reach the mailboxes standing at stiff, aluminum attention amid giddy yellow newspaper racks. Here begins the cold-surfaced road to town. We do not take it but wander instead to Mo's weathered, turn-of-the-century barn that sits cattycorner across from the mailboxes. I unfold my stool and sit in the open door at the barn's far end to see what feathered action there might be in the brushpiles and the maples decked with mistletoe. Sal uses her remarkable motor to investigate long-vacant stalls and the ghost-scents of animals, the horse and the decrepit Toggenburg nanny goat, that Mo used to keep here. After the barn-stop, we cross the road first to inspect the feeders and birdbath in a neighbor's yard and then to move on along the shore. The route home follows the wooden and concrete bulkheads upriver. Variations in our rounds depend on the time of day; the aim is to make the most of available light by keeping the sun at my back. Mornings, when the sun climbs over the woods that border the back fields, we head down the fence line toward the prickly pears; afternoons, when the sun's blaze is intensified by its reflection from the river, we reverse this track.

Translated into bird-terms, the rounds mean an almost daily survey of species present at the Point. Open woods with a fair number of moribund trees tempt the woodpeckers. Creek mouth, beach, and sandbar provide for gulls and waders. Reclusive birds that like dense cover tease us along the prickly pear path, fence line, and pond road; here blue-grey gnatcatchers construct lichen-covered nests no bigger than a demitasse, the migrating black-throated blue and Blackburnian warblers pause briefly in autumnal shadows, and the resident towhees sing vibrato or loudly call *hweet*. From the found-pier, the wide view of water and sky offers herons, dabbling ducks, and raptors—red-tailed hawks, Northern harriers, merlins, the ever-chirping osprey. The fields give birds that delight in open spaces—meadowlarks, swallows, and sparrows. At Mo's barn, I might see anything: a brown creeper ascending a tree trunk as if it were a spiral staircase, a wood thrush tugging at a sheet of trashed plastic and flying away with a scrap to install in its nest, a pair of great-crested flycatchers tucking pine straw and snakeskins under an eave for their nest. Everywhere on land, no matter what else may be happening, the Carolina wrens chide us with their calls. The river is bountiful with birds that fish for their livings—terns, double-crested cormorants, loons, diving ducks, the flap-and-glide brown pelicans that look like refugees from pterodactyl times.

As Sal and I make rounds, I become the Pied Piper of Great Neck Point. Our excursion is an alarm and a summons, waking every yard dog from its sleep and pulling it into our train. Sometimes the dogs dash ahead, sometimes they lag; they play or quarrel. And off we go, a roiling, noisy parade of woman, Doberman, chow, beagle, rottweiler, shepherd-mix, many black-Lab types, even more Brand-X mutts. I know some of them by name; strangers are designated by salient characteristics—Red Collar, Gimpy, Yellow Pup. Most of them, lacking Sally's good manners, don't know that human knees are not for pushing. But I rise from the dust or sand, shake myself off, and on we go pell-mell, like a traveling circus. Dog-birding: what kind of sport is this? We're bound to scare the birds.

But we don't. At least, the dogs don't, despite their thunderpaws and motormouths. As we wend our boisterous way down path, road, and fence line, I speculate why. Certainly, this free-flowing pack startles the birds and flushes the shyer ones from cover. The birds, however, quickly settle back; those flushed alight nearby. Only when they notice my presence do they vanish, wrapping themselves in a camouflage of stillness and silence. The dogs, perhaps, are seen as animals going about their own business, a business that does not include interfering with avian strategies for survival. Intrusive as the dogs are, their bigness, noise, and rollicking locomotion are not interpreted as serious threats. For all the birds seem to know, the dogs might be deer or bear or field mice. Why, then, do I come through as dangerous? Guns are not part of my bag-

26

gage, nor do I rob nests or compete for food. Awk-wardness may be the answer, sheer human awk-wardness, and the inability ever to be fully at home in the natural world. I cannot stop centering on self.

Luckily for my knees and noise-assaulted ears, the pack easily becomes bored or tired. The dogs lack not only Sally's manners but her pep. They're not reg-ularly innoculated or wormed; carrying around a load of internal parasites wears them out right quickly. The dogs drop out of the parade and head home to finish their naps. Sal knows *her* job. She trots onward by my side.

Her awareness of birds shows itself in several spe-cific ways. The summer laughing gulls and royal terns, the winter ring-billed, greater black-backed, and Bo-naparte's gulls flocked on the sandbar at creek mouth are fair game for chasing. She spots them and bounds forward, pronking through the shallow water as if it were a grassy plain and she an antelope. She plays an-other game with great blue herons. The playing field is front yard, bulkhead, and pier pilings. The hour is ei-ther dawn or well after dark. The game has no seasons. Sometimes heron sounds the starting whistle with its raucous call; sometimes dog issues a let-me-out-now scratch on the trailer's aluminum door. Even if heron is silent, dog knows the bird is out there, perched and beckoning. Dog rushes barking toward heron. Heron squawks, lazily spreads wings, and flies to another perch mere yards away. Barking, dog runs along the shore following heron. Heron squawks again and again flies to another nearby perch. Dog can become so ea-

27

ger—or incensed—that she jumps off the bulkhead and swims after heron as it flaps from piling to piling. The two occupy themselves with these maneuvers for two to ten minutes at a time. Calling a halt is the heron's prerogative; it ends the action by giving wings full spread and flying far out over the river. The game, if it is a game, is closed to other players. If heron becomes aware of the presence of a human being, it straightway disappears. Dawn after dawn, night after night, year after year, dog and heron engage in the contest. The same heron? Different birds and immature ones, I suspect, but I don't really know. I do know Sal's motives for indulging in such antic bird-play. She's enjoying herself, of course, but more important, she's driven by bone-bred instinct to defend her territory and banish the large intruder with the foghorn voice. The heron's motive? That one's up for grabs.

I want to see eagles. The desire is so intense that it pursues me into sleep; eagles soar through my dreams. A perilous condition: Wishes can so overheat imagination that a chicken looks like a phoenix.

We've plunged through the woods, Sal and I, heading creekward for a quick survey of the action. I'm rushing because it's nearly time to rattle pots and pans for supper; after a quarter of a century of training my children to expect their dinners promptly at six-thirty, I discover, now that they're adults responsible for the assuagement of their own appetites, that I've inexorably programmed my own stomach for the magic hour. But the pull of the creek counters rising pangs of hunger: springtime migrations are underway, and the cast of northbound shorebirds on the sandbar can change daily.

There they are, dainty semi-palmated plover, least sandpipers with legs of dull chartreuse, and another species of the little sandpipers known as peeps. Western or semi-palmated? The two are nearly identical. With choreographic precision, they run along the river-washed edges of the sandbar, pause, poke down their bills, and pull up minuscule reddish worms. Nothing out of the ordinary—except that on the fringes of the troupe of plover, something else runs, pauses, and pokes. It looks much like them—stubby bill, black necklace on a pale breast, but it's larger and the bill is all black, not orange dipped in soot: a lone Wilson's plover. Spotting the tiny dancers, Sal bounds eagerly through the shallows. They lift off, piping softly as they wheel away in tight, wing-to-wing formations.

Wilson's plover—I've not seen one here before. Now my stomach can take precedence. Dog and I head home down the prickly-pear path. Behind a lat-ticework of needlerushes and myrtle branches, the pond gleams like gilded silver. I scan the surface for wood ducks or a late-staying loon. Nothing ruffles the water, not bird nor jumping fish nor turtle's snout. And nothing calls or chirps from the underbrush beside the path, nothing flies overhead. The day seems to hover, to halt a moment before it resumes its dive to-ward sunset. I drop the binoculars and keep moving, keep looking pondward.

Wait!

29

Aerial movement over the trees at pond's far end. A shape soaring, descending, wholly dark against the late afternoon glare. What am I looking at? In this light, impossible to tell. It angles its huge wings like flaps, puts down landing gear, and settles on the top of the tallest tree, a baldy cypress jutting above the neighboring pines. The crown wears a small clutter of sticks—a nest that wasn't here last week. The bird flies off. I stand stock still. Soon it returns, gripping not a stick but a fair-sized log in its talons. It positions the log carefully on the clutter and tamps it down, weight on one leg, then the other, in the avian equivalent of a jig. Damn the westering sun! It strikes my vision at a right angle; its burning light steals color and turns the bird into a black silhouette. Sal leaps ahead while I trudge home. Eagle? Common sense says osprey.

Morning breaks fair and warm, but light for viewing is even worse, for the sun cresting the trees hits me square on from the left and lends its glitter to the pond's whole surface. All I can see is that not one but two enormous birds are continuing to airlift building materials to the top of the cypress. The nest grows visibly. What's needed for color, for sure identification of the twosome is a frontal approach straight across the pond. I enlist an ally, Bonnie, who has a day off from work. She's thoroughly pleased by an excuse to scrap housecleaning in favor of an outdoor expedition.

Sal tagging along, we tote a rubber raft and paddles through the woods. At the creek mouth, Sal indicates that under no circumstances will she embark in anything that feels so frail and wobbly underfoot. We're not unhappy about her decision; her claws could dig holes in the insubstantial fabric. Leaving her stretched in a damp, sandy hollow of her own digging, we wade the raft through the creek mouth, shove it over the sandbar at the entrance to the pond, and climb aboard.

Bonnie in the bow, we face forward, paddling the raft as if it were a canoe. No hurry, for we have all day to traverse the half-mile of barely ruffled water. Fish jump, and we know they're mullet because they leap across the water, splash-splash-splash, with the multiple jumps of skipping stones. A snapper with a head as big as my fist eyes us briefly and pulls its hooked beak underwater. Bearing their burdens, the two birds come and go, jigging each new timber neatly into place. Midway to the tree, I can see their gleaming heads. We paddle slowly on. Yes, the heads are definitely white. But when we near the tree, a closer look shows pale underwings with black wrist-patches and a dark eye-stripe on each bird's head. Only the foreheads, cheeks, and napes are white. Pandion's children, osprey after all. Yesterday I should have seen the tell-tale crook of the wings in flight, should have let common sense prevail.

"My God!" says Bonnie, looking back the way we've come. "What's *that*?"

I swivel. It's Sally. Her black-and-rust head cleaves the surface; water streams behind her in a long wake. Her breath comes out in hoarse, involuntary croaks. She's come half a mile, speed-swimming as if there were a gold medal at stake. No, not a medal but her life. We grab the paddles. She's only thirty feet away,

31

twenty, ten. Bonnie pulls the sodden, heavy bundle of fur and bones over the gunwale. In the workaday world, Bonnie is an emergency medical technician. Sal seems to know that. Groaning, shivering hard, she shuts her eyes and curls her large self into Bonnie's arms. I paddle home.

Osprey, eagles—who cares? We almost lose Sally. At home she crawls into the Chief's chair and does not eat or drink, does not stir except to blink her eyes and breathe. Face tight, chin trembling, the Chief prepares to mourn. Faithful, stupid dog! She knew that her kind does not want to swim and knew as well that swimming was the only way to reach her people. Twice we carry her to the car and make the fifty-mile round trip to the vet. He diagnoses exhaustion and muscle damage, rehydrates her, and urges us to tempt her appetite by doctoring kibble with otherwise forbidden morsels of people-food—lean hamburger, boned chicken. On the sixth day, Sal staggers from the chair to her dish, wolfs two cups of kibble seasoned with clam chowder, inhales the water in her bowl, and asks for seconds all around. The Chief unlocks his grim visage. In another week, Sal is romping along as I trek pondward with spotting scope to survey progress at the ospreys' nest. The strain put on her muscles by that desperate swim has left only one visible trace: when she wants to scratch, her left hindleg can't quite make connection with her ear.

In an ancient sense, I really have found eagles, or so Pliny the Elder assures me. Writing in the first century A.D. and calling them by their Greek name *haliaetus,* the Roman natural historian identified the osprey as one of six kinds of eagles. He describes well the sharp-eyed bird's lofty hover as it scans below for fish, its precipitous stoop to catch them, and the force with which its breast slices the water. He almost certainly observed osprey as they went about feeding themselves. He probably saw their nests. Long before Pliny, osprey were the objects of human attention; the Egyptians not only watched them but accorded some of them the honor of mummification and entombment. The species, to which many modern ornithologists assign not only a genus but a family of its own—Pandionidae, has immemorially fished and bred on every continent but Antarctica. On matters of breeding and rearing young, however, Pliny relays the marvelous rumors furnished him by a credulous world. All osprey, he writes, are hybrids, the result of cross-breeding with other kinds of eagles, and from the mating of these hybrids comes the smaller vultures, which in turn lay eggs that hatch out the great vultures, which do not breed at all. Translating almost word for word a tale told by Aristotle four centuries earlier, Pliny writes that *haliaetus* is unique among eagles in the method that it uses to sort worthy chicks from those not fit to hover, stoop, and seize their scaly prey. Beating its nestlings, the adult forces them to stare straight into the sun; if one should blink or its eyes begin to water, the grown bird casts it forthwith from the nest as "a bastard and a mongrel debasement of the breed." The chick that keeps its eyes firm on the sun is reared.

Pliny also refers to the bird by an early version of

33

the name it bears today—*ossifraga,* bone-breaker, which time and the tricks of linguistic change have transformed first to *osfraie,* then osprey. But unlike the marrow-eating vultures of the Old World, osprey have never been known to crack bones. But then, the Romans and the Greeks regularly and indiscriminately lumped together the hawks, eagles, and vultures and often used one categorical term to mean any of the others.

Many raptors and scavengers are superficially alike in that they soar imperiously, possess fierce miens, and dine on flesh. Another of Pliny's six "eagles" almost surely qualifies from his description as a harrier, no eagle but a long-tailed, long-winged hawk. Still another may be the golden eagle, which has from prehistoric times populated Mediterranean countries as well as North America, but precise identification cannot be extracted from Pliny's passing mention.

Around the world, long before Pliny, long before the Greeks told the story of Pandion, osprey fished, built their bulky nests, and reared nestlings that were invariably osprey, not vultures great or small. And here, before any person set foot on the shore where I now live, the osprey must have flourished. At Great Neck Point, we can trace the human presence from the artifacts we find: old bricks and iron from the nineteenth-century farming days; ballast stones and the bottoms of handblown rum and gin bottles from the days of sail; glazed fragments of crude colonial-era chamberpots; the shards of clay pots manufactured by Indians in the Middle Woodland Period two millenia ago; the projectile point that may have been flaked from red jasper as long ago as 8000 B.C. The present inhabitants of the Point are merely the latest in a long procession that may have begun its march and seen the osprey of this rivershore ten thousand years before our day.

It took a while for North Carolina to find its own Pliny, but nearly three hundred years ago he appeared in the person of John Lawson, Surveyor General to the British Lords Proprietors of Carolina. In 1709, Lawson published a rhapsodic book, *A New Voyage to Carolina,* meant to entice fellow Britons into crossing the Atlantic for a new world, a "Summer-Country," in which all life's needs would be met by the teeming waters and the fertile lands. One chapter furnishes a natural history that minutely lists and describes vegetation, beasts and birds, fish and shellfish. Nor does Lawson forget the creatures he calls "Insects"—alligators, snakes, frogs, and lizards. He relegates "Reptiles, or smaller Insects" such as butterflies and beetles to an apologetic paragraph in which he excuses himself for not writing the large volume that their "innumerable Quantities" deserve.

Lawson begins his catalogue of avian species found in Summer-Country with the bald eagle because it is "reckon'd the King of Birds." Second-listed is the golden eagle, which he calls "gray" and dismisses in a single, non-descriptive sentence because it is familiar to his British readers. The King is treated at much greater length, and Lawson shines here as Pliny *redivivus*. Like

35

mistletoe clumped high in a maple tree, fable clings airy and parasitic to the sturdy limbs of fact:

The first [bird] I shall speak of, is the bald Eagle, so call'd because his Head, to the middle of his Neck, and his Tail, is white as Snow. These birds continually breed the Year round; for when the young Eagles are just down'd, with a sort of woolly white feathers, the Hen-Eagle lays again, which Eggs are hatched by the Warmth of the young ones in the Nest, so that the Flight of one Brood makes Room for the next, that are but just hatch'd. They prey on any living thing they can catch. They are heavy of Flight, and cannot get their Food by Swiftness. . . . The bald Eagle attends the Gunners in Winter, with all the Obsequiousness imaginable, and when he shoots and kills any Fowl, the Eagle surely comes in for his Bird, and besides, those that are wounded, and escape the Fowler, fall to the Eagle's share. He is an excellent Artist at stealing young Pigs, which Prey he carries alive to his Nest, at which time the poor Pig makes such a Noise over Head, that Strangers that have heard them cry, and not seen the Bird and his Prey, have thought there were Flying Sows and Pigs in that Country. The Eagle's Nest is made of Twigs, Sticks, and Rubbish. It is big enough to fill a handsome Carts Body, and commonly so full of nasty Bones and Carcasses that it stinks most offensively. This Eagle is not bald, till he is one or two years old.

In truth, the eagle begins to acquire its snowy head at the age of three; at four, the head becomes entirely white. The bird may also breed for the first time in its fourth year, but never—not ever—has one batch of nestlings incubated the next. The work of raising one brood a year is quite enough. As for Obsequiousness to Gunners, Lawson mistakes the bird's behavior and motives, but he has a point: the eagle does not disdain good birds that waterfowl hunters have failed to retrieve or simply killed for sport. Nor, according to Lawson, are Gunners the only servitors that cater to its appetite; the eagle depends also on the osprey's skill: "[T]here is a Fishawk that catches Fishes, and suffers the Eagle to take them from her, although she is long-wing'd and a swift Flyer, and can make far better way in her Flight than the Eagle can. . . . The Fishing Hawk is the Eagle's Jackal, which most commonly (though not always) takes his Prey for him." Not so. Bald eagles have been known to skyjack other eagles' prey—and perhaps carry away a piglet or two but never a sow, and though they've worked their aerial piracies on osprey, the practice is downright rare. Osprey and bald eagles coexist peaceably in the same riparian habitats, with neither species infringing on the other's livelihood.

I keep watch on the nest-building on the far side of the pond and watch the pair as they go about the other business of their lives. Their fishing is a wonder: the downward plummet from a hover or a glide, the whole bird—not just its legs and breast—cleaving water and disappearing, the rise into air with talons clenched on a fish that's always held face forward. After the first few yards of flight, the wingbeats seem to falter as if the weight of new-caught prey were dragging the captor back toward the water; the bird is simply shaking water from its feathers. One day, I watch an osprey land with its fish, a croaker, on a

37

cypress limb. Perching on one foot, with the other it holds the croaker to its sharp-hooked bill and eats as if it were munching on a drumstick. Later, on the sand beneath a pine upriver from the creek, I find remnants of other dinners. Like the other raptors and the owls, osprey regurgitate the indigestible portion of their meals. Birds that prey on mammals or other birds cast out bones neatly encased in fur or feathers, but osprey package their pellets in sequins—fish scales that glitter in the sunlight bounding off sand and water on the far side of Courts Creek.

Five weeks and two days after the first sight of the nest, I watch as an osprey descends feet-first into the pond and rises not with a fish but a mat of fine green pondweed in its sure grasp. The weed is lifted to the nest: soft lining for eggs about to be laid. The osprey could have chosen other materials to cushion its chicks. A magpie among raptors, it is apparently programmed to delight in nest-decorating schemes that feature an eclectic taste in trash. Nests are sometimes fitted out like playpens, containing all manner of objects from natural cast-offs, such as shells, to human leavings— clothes and toys, bottles and fishing line. At Courts Creek, the nesting pair can select from a supermarket of litter. River and shore produce oyster, clam, and mussel shells, barnacled driftwood, and tarpon scales as tough as horn and twice the size of silver dollars. Generations of river-dwellers and boaters might also provide the proper gewgaws for a nest. The osprey could indulge in period furnishings—a potsherd or a piece of chamberpot. Or they could opt for modern—a scrap of treadless tire, detergent jugs in a multitude of designs and chemically unfading colors, electric insulators, aluminum cans still bearing legible brand-names for every beer now brewed, a pair of nearly new childsized jeans, or soda bottles formed from glass or plastic.

Activity continues unabated on the far side of the pond. The grown birds depart and return; the nest is as busy as an airport. When the water is low and the light comes from the west, I wade the creek mouth to watch the osprey from the sandbar at pond's riverward end. Sal pronks along. She has not attempted another record-setting dog-paddle, but in the hot and sweaty doldrums of summer, she voluntarily leaps into the river to cool off. And there she swims as eagerly as any Labrador retriever.

Not quite two months after the lining of the nest, three heads lift above its rim to watch the approach of a fish-bearing parent. I announce the glad news to Bonnie and the Chief and propel them pondward to see for themselves.

Bird-sounds change with the seasons. Autumn: common loons wail and yodel, waterfowl take flight in a slapping rush, the wings of migrant songbirds make faint drumrolls on the dark skin of night. Winter: lone red-tailed hawks scream overhead while thronging sparrows scratch at brittle leaves and hosts of yellow-rumped warblers chip-chip-chip incessantly from the myrtles. The only song is that of the Carolina wren—bright melodies far larger than the throats from which they issue. Spring: song rises filling night and day as each male volubly proclaims his right to a breeding ground where food is assured for future young or ample, species-enhancing opportunities for sex present themselves. Summer: laughing gulls on the pilings and sandbar squeal, great blue herons tear night's fabric with raucous calls, the won't-quit wrens keep hollering, but the loudest sound is no sound at all. Mute throats and closed bills protect the nest-locations and the new-hatched young as adult birds go about the gaunt work of stuffing baby craws.

And in the summer period of silence I see the phoenix. Not chicken, not hawk nor vulture nor osprey, but phoenix, and I realize that we have been seeing it all along. The problem is that I have been looking not for a sign but for a shape, a particular configuration of body parts arranged in particular color-combinations and the particular active and passive postures that pen and brush can draw, that camera can capture with utmost precision. A sign, however, can't be put on a shelf for future reference or toted in my bird-bag along with insect repellent and knife. The sign has been present at the creek since the time of territory-claiming birdsong, when the marsh wrens burbled from the needlerushes and the red-winged blackbirds clung to slender stalks of cordgrass to uncoil their tightly wound, metallic tunes. It was present when the royal terns were copulating on the sandbar, wings pumping and open bills emitting a shrill *whoo-whoo-whoo*. It was present when the gulls and terns were flocked on the sandbar quiescent, heads facing into a light southwest

40

wind. The large dark bird that we have seen irregularly during the spring, the bird dismissed as one more osprey on a fishing trip, flies out of the creek again and, as before, panics the resting gulls and terns into instantaneous, soundless flight. The dark bird, ignoring the wheeling, white explosion, heads downriver. I see its classic shape and the flat, perfectly horizontal plane of its broad wings. And I read the sign we've overlooked. When an osprey flies out of the creek, when Sally gives chase, when other events trigger the shorebirds' flight, they squeal and caw and scold. But when this eagle comes, juvenile though it is, for unknown purposes the shorebirds hold their tongues. It's not the silence, however, that affords safety from the perceived predator but the flock's densely packed, whirling confusion. An eagle cannot single out an individual bird on which to pounce.

Yes, eagles are summering up the ancestral creek and elsewhere on our portion of the Neuse. When we've learned what to look for, we see them not every day but often enough to shore up a sometimes doubt-stricken faith in their presence. And sightings become more frequent. One cold April morning at daybreak, Dorothy telephones: "Creek—eagle on sandbar." I neither thank her nor say goodbye. I hang up, put the hot skillet on a cold burner, seize binoculars, and run. Oh yes! A big brown youngling stands at water's edge, its body horizontal atop feather-plump legs. It's eating a fish. Two dozen crows bombard it with a black yammer and flapping wings. The eagle pays this silliness no heed. Then, on a hot June evening, Bonnie reports the first eagle she's ever laid eyes on, an adult perched in a tree three miles from the Point on the road to town. It took wing as she approached, flew across the road, and zoomed at low altitude down a logging trail straight as a runway. "So huge," she says, "it almost blotted out the sun."

The eagles may be transient, but they're here—the erratic forays out of the creek; the juveniles hunkered down atop road-killed 'possums on the road to town; the first-year adult, its head snowy, its tail still tarnished with immature soot, that sails at treetop level over the back fields; the mature eagle, incandescent in the sun, that bathes and preens on the marginal sands of a marshy island upriver. The eyrie remains vacant.

Will a new nest take massive shape there amid the lesser constructs of the osprey? Or in some nearby wetland less populated by other birds? Will eagles even continue to summer here?

Faith cries for an affirmative answer. Doubt says, Rejoice in eagles while ye may. I'm not a pessimist, but doubt has reason on its side. The eagle-friendly wilderness around us is literally under the axe. In bird-silent summer we have heard the thwack of blades on standing timber and the laughing, cursing voices of the axemen as they clear the timber plantations for real-estate developments. Along the half-mile of shore just upriver from Courts Creek, along the creek mouth and the pond itself, they have cut through the thickets of honeysuckle and greenbriar, felled slow-growing live oaks, and spared some spindly pines and sweet gums. The needlerushes on the far side of creek and pond

have been given a crew cut. We've heard the earth-
chewing roar of heavy equipment, and through the
torn veil of forest we've seen the yellow behemoths
that gouged, graded, and paved the development's
roads. Two lots close to the creek sport SOLD signs
that I can read through binoculars from the found-pier
on our side of the pond.

Early on, two pairs of osprey were evicted from the
high-dollar riverfront lots where they had squatted.
They'd each chosen a dead tree within feet of the water
and begun to crown it with the matchstick rudiments
of a nest. Both trees tumbled in the axemen's first on-
slaught. One pair may have moved upcreek to the
colony surrounding the abandoned eyrie. I know
where the other pair chose to rear its brood—in the
nest atop the cypress on the far side of the pond, the
nest I watched a-building from almost the first log.
The earth has turned around the sun four times since
that miraculous summer. The following year no osprey used the nest; battered by the high winds of
winter storms, it became dilapidated, its sticks project-
ing up, down, sideways like Slovenly Peter's unkempt
hair. But in the very next turning of the earth, after the
riverfront nests had been destroyed, osprey rebuilt and
refurbished the tousled ruin. A pair has not only occupied the nest since then but added to it. The construct is now at least six feet deep and so massive that I
wonder how one slender tree can bear its weight.
These days, Sal and I can leave the trailer, wade the
creek, crunch through the stubble of dead vines and
saplings, and reach the paved road in fifteen ambling

43

minutes, far less time than it took for Bonnie and me to paddle the length of the pond. Two more minutes, and we can cross Lot 3 to pond's edge and stand beneath the huge nest. The osprey utter no soft chirps this time. While one of the pair circles silently, warily overhead, the other curses us in high-pitched shrieks—*kreekreekreekreekree*—till we return to the road.

No human being has yet laid foundations for any house in the development. Lot 3 is not yet sold. But even when the masons and the carpenters come in, the osprey may well continue to rear their broods atop the cypress. Pandion's children tolerate the human presence with remarkable nonchalance; they will nest within spitting distance of our habitations, care for their young, and go about their fishing unperturbed. Eagles are more skittish.

I learn at last that I haven't really been looking for eagles after all. Or, that looking has simply been an excuse to go on quest for something larger and more tantalizing. I may never stub my toe on the pot of gold, but I have seen rainbow colors indicating that it does exist: colors too many to count in a bewilderment of shapes that speak in ten thousand tongues and silences, that move most agilely or maintain most dignified stasis. As dazzling with wonder as the way of an eagle in the air are the ways of osprey, woodpeckers, and swans, of toads, snakes, and fire ants, of fish and jellies and isopods and the other creatures of the river and the Point. They live, reproduce, and die according to commandments encapsulated in their genes. Their populations rise and fall with amazing overall stability. At ease in open spaces or packed into the least crevices of earth, air, and water, they know the places to which instinct and long evolution have appointed them.

I and my two-footed, ham-fisted kind are the only creatures on earth that have scratched and climbed our way out of the hunting-gathering niche for which we were designed, in which we stayed till domestication of plants and animals gave us the seeming liberty to thumb our noses at the rest of life. Die in childbirth, die of savaging by bear-claws? No thanks. Medicine and supermarkets are addictive habits impossible to kick.

I'm really looking for my properly respectful human place in the old, bubbling, steamy, fragrant stew. With a little luck and a lot more *kairos,* maybe we'll all find it.

Toad-in-the-Hole

Toad-in-the-hole, metaphoric version: a slice of bread with an egg plopped into its cut-out center and fried golden-brown in butter, a breakfast demanded with enthusiastic regularity by my children when they attended elementary school. Toad-in-the-hole, literal version: *Bufo terrestris,* a Southern toad squatting sedately in a small dark cavern at the base of a backyard sweet gum tree. Ample dimensions indicate gender: female, the size of my fist. Day after day, spring into summer, we see her warty, beige-and-brown body framed by shadows and grey bark. Sometimes she retreats as we pass on our way to the shed; more often she stays in place, pop-eyed and aloof, her creamy throat pulsing above her lightly freckled chest. Sally, fascinated by the toads that hop like wind-up toys through the yard at night, pays no mind to this immobile specimen. Good thing. We do not let her play with toads, for the wart-like bumps of any species secrete a poison that can sicken and sometimes kill an aggressor.

The toad, a benign and placid insect-eating creature, has suffered widespread theft of its reputation and good name. *Bufo,* once the Romans' general word for a toad and now the scientific designation for its genus, pops up harum-scarum as *buffoon,* a clowning, ludicrous figure. The everyday word appears in darker incarnations: *toadstool,* a generic designation for any lethal mushroom; *toady,* a contraction of toad-eater, a charlatan's apprentice who pretends to ingest the creature's poison and spew it forth unharmed, or a person who conceals malice beneath fawning words and deeds. Toad: an innocent being but, by age-old accusation, the cause of warts in all who touch its rough, dry skin. Toad: basic ingredient of evil potions. Ben Jonson wrote of toads, owls' eyes, and bats' wings that "These also, both in confessions of Witches, and the testemonye of writers, are of principal use in theyr witchcraft." And Shakespeare's toad in *As You Like It* contains a powerful magic:

> Sweet are the uses of adversity,
> Which like the toad, ugly and venomous,
> Wears yet a precious jewel in his head. . . .

The jewel, a charm against poison, is a toadstone, a substance actually of diverse origins but so named because its colors resemble those of the toad in whose head it was thought to have accreted. Nonsense! The toad has never worn anything in its head but brains and the usual organs of good sense and life-support.

In our real back yard, we see a not-imaginary toad. Resting in her cool, dim hollow, she seems a tutelary presence. Toad: a small, plump, self-possessed, quite tangible representative of something we cannot see—a poetry of amphibians, an idea of order in Great Neck Point.

One summer morning she is gone. Night-long rains have drenched the fields and woods, but dawn has come in blue and fresh. Sally and I make our rounds to music, a chorus of chirrs and trills that sometimes rises to a crescendo startling as a siren. The wheel-ruts on the pond road brim with rainwater and Southern toads. The females have spread themselves into flat, blunt-pointed stars, and each is spraddled by a greeny-brown male less than half her size. The males cling lustily to female backs and wait to shed their sperm on the two long, jelly-coated egg-strings that each mate will lay. And, oh, the females are transformed. No longer dressed in modest brown and beige, they've put on bridal finery of flaming orange, with wide black bracelets abundantly encircling every leg. I am not pre-pared for this sight. Certainly, mating colors are men-tioned somewhere on the pallid pages of textbooks, but the amateur guides on our shelves neither picture nor describe such a marvel of excited gaudiness. I learn later that brilliance has always lurked beneath the skin's dull surface. Pores responding to the erotic moment have opened wide to let these fires blaze.

Toad-out-of-the-hole: an absence occasioned by having to go about life's main work of reproduction. After the rain and the musical morning, she does not return to her shelter at the base of the sweet gum tree. Real hole, real tree, but toad becomes a creature of imagination, of memory. She's done her part, however, to increase the chances for another tenant next year. Meanwhile, my children feed their sons and daughters the metaphoric breakfast.

The Menhaden's Nursemaid

"C'mere!" our neighbor Tom shouts as I leave the trailer, bucket in hand, to haul my crabpots. He stands at water's edge next door to extract fish from the gill nets he's just brought ashore from an overnight stay in the river. The sun is cresting the trees to the east.

Crabs can wait. I race across the shallow drainage ditch that separates our yard from his. What will it be this time? An ardent fisherman, he helps to satisfy my quenchless curiosity about the river's children by saving the oddities that sometimes tangle themselves in his nets: inshore lizardfish; Atlantic filefish; fingerling cobia; sea robin with pectoral fins like the wings of a sailplane; lookdown, small, flat-bodied, and as round and silvery as its namesake—*selena,* Greek for a moongoddess and the moon itself.

"Ever seen this?" Tom holds out a square, brown plastic tub.

It contains a dead menhaden, an all too familiar species that casts itself overabundantly into our summer nets. When the menhaden are schooling in our part of the river, we throw back ten or twenty for every edible fish we keep. This one measures about nine inches from stem to stern, on the large side for the river.

"Looky here," Tom says, pointing to the menhaden's open mouth.

"Oh, m'goodness, what *is* it?" Something plump and white as a grub is wriggling itself into the light. It looks like a medieval drawing come to life: the pallid soul escaping from a corpse's mouth.

"Don't know rightly what it's called, but what it does is help the menhaden process food. There's a deficiency, you see, in the menhaden's digestive system. All of 'em have these helpers."

My curiosity is thirstier than ever. The inch-long creature emerging from the dead menhaden's mouth has a fat, bleached, slightly repulsive but undeniable reality. Tom's explanation for its presence, however, seems like a chip off the folklore block, a tale kin to that of cooked eel turning raw if left in the refrigerator overnight. (Improper cleaning is the grain of fact around which that pearl has accreted.) The Chief and I have tugged many dead and dying menhaden from our net, I've saved them for crabpot bait, and not once has either of us seen this ghostly grub.

The crabpots wait a little longer, till I've checked the guide to near-shore marine life. The book gives modest help, indicating generally that the grub is a cymothoid, one of a large family of parasitic isopods. I'm not satisfied. I start asking questions.

52

"Sure," says Al, "the menhaden's nursemaid, that's what you're talking about." But he doesn't know how the nursemaid goes about its duties nor how it got hired in the first place. He does, however, show me how to spot menhaden when they're schooling close inshore.

On summer evenings they announce themselves by their noise. It's not the crisp *pop-pop-pop* of shrimp nor the ripple-making splash of an airborne mullet or shad as it returns to the water. It's a gentle but incessant murmur, a rustling whisper, made by myriad mouths breaking the surface for an instant and instantly retreating. The sound brings bad news and good: in the morning we'll be cussing as we extricate one menhaden after another from the net and pitch them back, and we'll be blessing the larger fish—blues, maybe!—that snared themselves in pursuit of a menhaden dinner. Some people sell their menhaden as crabpot bait, but at two cents a pound, it takes a heap of menhaden to make a dollar.

Though people don't eat them (at least not yet), menhaden support fleets of commercial vessels that spread their nets in rivermouths and sounds to herd in precisely this species. The catch is processed for oil that's used in paint and cosmetics or ground into fertilizer and chicken feed. (Have you ever wondered why some supermarket chicken tastes not like fowl but fish? Blame the menhaden.) It may be that menhaden will soon make the leap from chicken trough to china plates. Researchers now experiment with mashing parts of menhaden to make *surimi,* the fish-paste developed by the Japanese and currently manufactured from

53

other species to mold the "sea legs" that look like king crab legs but sell for half the price of the real thing.

The menhaden trap themselves in our nets because of their feeding habits. They swim with mouths wide open, letting a hearty broth of plankton flow through their buccal cavities and out through the gills, which are equipped with rakers—fine, feathery sieves—that strain all the goodies out of the soup. It's the gaping mouths that land the menhaden in trouble with nylon monofilament. River people say that menhaden "swallow the net." Or they try to, closing their mouths on the mesh and catching it in the hinges of their jaws. River people also call them "back-out fish." Instead of pulling them headfirst through the net like croaker or small bluefish, we must grasp them behind the gills and give a backward tug.

I keep asking questions about the nursemaid. Do all menhaden give lodging to these isopods? At what cost? Who pays and who profits? "Nursemaid" does not seem to designate a parasite; it sounds beneficent, implying a caretaking function, perhaps like that of an adult animal regurgitating pre-digested food for its young. Is there some substance to the talk about a defect in the menhaden's digestive system? And how does the nursemaid arrive on the scene? I put the question to fishermen on and off the river and to the owners of seafood markets. They're familiar with the nursemaid, but they have no satisfying answers.

The person who can lead me to the facts appears on an August afternoon—a slender, dark-haired man behind a table at a seafood exhibition. A two-foot-long fish, a small sandbar shark, lies on the table, and the man is giving a hands-on demonstration of how to clean the shark properly and prepare it for cooking. I've been asking all the exhibitors about the nursemaid, and one of them finally said, "You might check over there with Joe." Joe's nametag identifies him more fully as Joseph W. Smith, National Marine Fisheries Service. And, hallelujah, all I need say is "menhaden" and "isopod" before one answer is found.

"*Olencira praegustator,* that's your critter," he says.

Praegustator—an apt name for something that lives in the mouth of something else. It means "foretaster," the one that takes the first sampling of the food put on the table.

Joe adds that he doesn't know all that much about the critter, his work as a fisheries biologist centers elsewhere, but, come to think of it, he's read about this very isopod in a specialized journal. Would I like a copy of the article?

Praise be to those whose memories are like gillrakers, collecting nourishing particles of odd information and letting the dross go. Six days later, the article, published more than fifteen years ago, arrives in the mailbox. It tells a strange story.

When *O. praegustator* leaves the incubation of its mother's brood-pouch, it begins life as a free-swimming male. After it finds a female and mates, it looks for lodging in a juvenile menhaden that has no other tenant. The fish's open, indiscriminate mouth sweeps in isopod along with food, and both travel to the gills, where the isopod fastens itself and enters a transitional

55

phase. No one knows if the isopod feeds directly on the gills or simply ingests the food trapped there. The host can sustain damage, sometimes massive but not often fatal, to all parts of its gills, from rakers to coverings. While the isopod occupies the gills, it undergoes a sex-change: roving male is transformed to sedentary female. When the change is complete, the isopod moves to the host's mouth and, facing forward, attaches itself to the roof. Snugged in, it apparently ceases to bite the host that feeds it and takes on its role as a taster. Like a cook testing an entrée before serving, isopod gets first crack at plankton-soup. The menhaden's gills heal. Fish and isopod assume a kind of commensal relationship. The isopod, no longer truly parasitic, has found armor for its soft body and issued itself another ticket for free meals; the fish, relieved of further injury, can easily support this uninvited mouthful of a guest. At this point, though only one party gains, neither is hurt.

No, nothing is wrong with the menhaden's digestive tract. Nor does the fish need the isopod to perform any other everyday task. And, no, not every juvenile menhaden is so infested. *O. praegustator* shuns cooler waters; menhaden off the Massachusetts coast don't encounter these hitchhikers. Only in the Chesapeake and waters farther south do these isopods appear regularly in numbers ranging from slight to moderate but never in such hordes that they adversely affect the menhaden fisheries.

A commensal relationship—what a homey word *commensalism* is! It suggests comfort, courtesy, and enough mouth-watering food to fill every belly. It

56

means "tabled together," sharing the same heaping board. I think of noonday farm dinners—three meats with gravy, five kinds of vegetable, homemade biscuits, and sweet-potato pie. Those dining together may be strangers without mutual customs, language, and interests, but they gather at the common board in a common cause—the need to fuel themselves so that they can go about their main business. To make the picture truly commensal, place a few other species at the table with the people—a chicken, a horse, a beetle, all minding their manners in a domestic version of the Peaceable Kingdom. The main business of this motley crew may appear in different guises—harvesting the corn, cleaning the barn—but underneath it's always the same: ensuring the future of each species at the table.

Menhaden and isopod tabled together look to me like a model of uneasy but workable companionship. As for my kind, here we are, stuck in the world's craw. And if we do not still cradle the notion that we are divinely appointed landlords exercising dominion over the planet, we may well think of ourselves as caretakers—nursemaids, if you will—for all that shelters, feeds, and clothes us and lets us get on with perpetuating ourselves in ever greater numbers. And all the while, we're really just bumbling onward, merrily tripping over our own feet, not knowing where we're headed.

Does the planet need us? The menhaden doesn't need its isopod and would be better off without it. The nursemaid that is not a nursemaid depends on the menhaden for its very life, and it knows enough to back off before it kills its host. But it operates on instinct. We must use our wits.

The Wind-Egg

〈〈〈-〈〈〈-〈〈〈-〈〈〈-〈〈〈-〈〈〈-〈〈〈-〈〈〈-〈〈〈-〈〈〈-〈〈〈-〈〈〈-〈〈〈-〈〈〈-〈〈〈-〈〈〈

Whir-r-r-r-rr. Wind whistles through wing feathers on an ascending scale. The noise is that of a soft cry, tremulous, almost petulant. For the second day in a row, a mourning dove has flown from the Gordian knot of honeysuckle and greenbriar that hangs from the lower branches of a pine. With Sal, I'm on my way to put a letter in our rural-route mailbox. Sal spots a cottontail and hares after it. I pause. Late spring: the Point's birds have turned serious attention to the production of more birds. This knot hides a nest, I'm sure of it. And there it is, a sprawling, rickety hodgepodge of sticks and twisted bits of dead grey vines, all suspended on live vine-stems in a dim green cavern of leaves. It looks loose, jerrybuilt, but the doves know exactly what they're doing. Sal, however, doesn't have the fuzziest idea of what she's doing. As always, she's lost her canny quarry but, nose to the ground, she's still in dogged pursuit, chasing that rabbit backwards in the direction from which it ran.

Great Neck Point offers a full selection of courses in bootstrap natural history, complete with field trips. I've signed up for a good many of them, and when the homework becomes an overload, as it regularly does, I've only hyperkinetic curiosity to blame. Bird-watching 101: the grand list for the Point has spilled from a scribbled page in the back of the field guide to a page in the front—one hundred and ninety-four species seen within half a mile of home. Will the list top two hundred? I keep prowling. Basic meteorology: spring and autumn cold fronts deposit migrating birds in the woods and brushpiles, and a change in wind-direction affects not only the migrators but the kinds of fish that swarm into our nets. Ichthyology includes not only identifying the catch but also dissections, known locally as "dressing fish"; the latter can keep us up till the wee hours. River, pond, and creek also schedule other lessons in aquatic life—crabs, jellyfish, isopods. On land, there's botany, pines to poison ivy; herpetology, garter and green snakes to timber rattlers; entomology, butterflies and beetles. Nor are the arachnids scanted; without warning or volition, I've suffered several crash courses in chiggers and ticks. School makes not the slightest provision for weekends or vacations, unless it rains. Even then, a downpour finds me poring over field guides. By some odd parthenogenesis, books breed books. The Chief keeps building shelves to hold the burgeoning collection.

This spring, an intensive seminar, with more books, has been added to the curriculum: nests. A squib in the newspaper relayed the Museum of Natural Science's request for volunteers to assist in compiling the state's Breeding Bird Atlas. What species nest in North Carolina, and where, and how? All fifty states are or have been engaged in such a five-year project. Some have completed an Atlas; others have barely started sending people out to peer into the underbrush and crane their necks toward higher reaches of the trees. In all innocence, I offered to help. The mail soon brought a fat manila envelope. My over-the-shoulder tote bag gained weight: bird book, knife, repellent, and collecting bags have been joined by maps and instructions; field-data sheets and three-by-five cards for recording details on each nest discovered. Such record-keeping forces the observer to note not just a bird, a nest, a clutch of eggs but their total context. From what materials is the nest built? How lined? How high off the ground? Amid precisely what surroundings—conifers, deciduous trees, mixed woods, fields? If the nest lies in a cavity, what compass-direction does the entrance-hole face? I'm being made to look at ways of life as well as living objects.

The nest snugged in vines and green leaf-light is the second dove's nest found this season. I stand nearby and begin a new card: MOURNING DOVE #2. Card's front is marked with the requisite information on context and the back with a brief note on the date, the time of day, and the action at the nest—adult flushed.

After robins, this kind of dove is the first species I was taught to identify. From the vantage point of a spectator, my memory looks back and sees the five-year-old girl arriving for breakfast in the dining room

61

of her grandfather's summer house. Her father, an up-with-the-dawn man, stands by the deep bay window that stretches across the entire north end of the room. His fried eggs, toast, and orange juice have long gone down the hatch. "Come, listen," he says, and she joins him at the window, framed on its exterior by trumpet vines. "That cooing—it's a mourning dove. Look close inside the vines, you'll see the nest." She doesn't see the nest, for it's well hidden, but she hears the dove's soft burbling and will ever after be able to summon the sound even when it's produced only by mind's ear rather than a live dove. It's not a sad song, not a lamentation, but a gently fretful flutter. Her father points out a dove perched on a nearby branch, and ever after not only its cooing but its posture and colors will be printed on memory. The house, renovated and made fit for winter use, will become her father's, and every spring thereafter, until she herself flies that Dutch colonial nest, she will notice doves nesting within the trumpet vines outside the bay window. Perhaps they still do.

Sal returns from her harebrained chase and nudges my hand: Hey, c'mon, let's get moving. En route to the mailbox, I check the grass basket that orchard orioles have woven and suspended from twigs amid the tip-top leaves of a pear tree; no birds at home today. I check the cavity that a pair of chickadees excavated in a dead stump two months ago. Taking turns to drill a sharply downsloping hole, they crammed their bills with minuscule wood-chips that they would spit into a scattering breeze from a perch five feet away. Today, one parent flies from the hole bearing in its bill a neatly packaged sac of nestling-feces—no sluttish housekeeping here. The young will soon be fledged.

After the out-going letter is deposited and the flag on the mailbox stood at red attention, we go to see what's happening with MOURNING DOVE #1. I see the shine of an unblinking, wary eye. An incubating bird sits motionless in the center of the nest. There's something new here: a white egg rests untended on the nest's rim.

A neighbor found this nest a week ago. Walking through her yard, she'd disturbed a snake, which fled into the wooded tangle on yard's perimeter. Her eye followed the snake into the underbrush, looked up, and met the dove's eye. The nest, a lattice of sticks, reposes deep in viny darkness guarded by thorns like Sleeping Beauty's castle. Today, on the edge of the wooded tangle, a black racer, perhaps the very snake that led my neighbor's glance toward the dove, lies like a slack cord along a woody stem.

That egg on the rim—from the fourth century B.C., Aristotle tells what it is: not a true egg at all but a wind-egg. Such eggs, he states, are laid without prior copulation; they are smaller, less tasty, and more liquid than those produced by a mated bird. Their contents never "coagulate" properly into yellow yolks surrounded by white. Though summer is the peak period for wind-eggs, they may also be laid in spring, when they're called zephyr-eggs because in that season some female birds have been seen facing into the inseminating wind with bills agape. Hen-birds of many species

allow themselves to be so fertilized by wind—
chickens, geese, and peahens, partridges and doves.
Writing centuries after Aristotle, the Roman Pliny says
that the third egg of a clutch laid by a pigeon or a dove
is invariably a wind-egg. (Pigeons—Pliny disagrees
with Aristotle's assessment of their character and cred-
its them with utmost modesty and unimpeachable
marital fidelity; he has never observed fooling around
in pigeon nests. He adds that males may succumb to
fits of pecking jealousy but later make amends to their
mates with much billing and cooing. Aristotle has no
truck with such romantic twaddle; in his book pigeons
are incurably lascivious. Great Neck Point, however, is
not the place to test the validity of either opinion;
we're too remote from pavement and roost-worthy
buildings to attract the fancy of rock-doves, as ornithologists politely refer to pigeons. Only three times
have I seen a pigeon at the Point, twice blown into our
yard by a hard storm, once strutting up the precipitous
roof of Dorothy's house. I told her she was ruining our
country neighborhood with city birds.)

The reason for the classical brooding on wind-eggs
may be simply that Greek philosopher and Roman natural historian were attempting to explain the enduring
fact of infertile eggs. Pliny's assertion that the third egg
is always a wind-egg may have arisen from the entirely
accurate observations that many birds, including
males, stand open-billed into the wind and that doves
and pigeons normally lay two eggs—and only two—in
each clutch. Rarely do these birds produce a third. To
the ancient mind, its appearance might have seemed

quite extraordinary, and when such an egregious event occurs, then surely its cause is supernatural. What better instrument than unseen wind to sire an empty egg?

Is the cold egg on nest's rim a third egg? I cannot see well enough into the briar-guarded darkness to tell how many eggs are being kept warm by the soft, featherless brood-patch on the belly of dove number one. The bird I see this morning is probably the male; with mourning doves, he generally takes the daytime shift while she does night duty. Somehow, in their joint thrust toward propagation, they must have sensed that one of their eggs would never hatch. In practical fashion, they've written off that small, elliptical effort and rolled it aside. I make a note of the rim-egg on the record card. The bird on the nest does not stir, nor does the black racer drooping from the woody stem.

On the way back to the trailer, I check the mockingbirds' nest tucked deep inside a clump of red-flowered trumpet honeysuckle. Occupied yesterday, it's vacant this morning—a chance now to inspect its construction. Conventional foundation of twigs, conventional lining of fine, dried grasses but, good grief, these mockers were the ultimate recyclers of the tackiest human trash. As their prime building material, they've chosen weathered cigarette filters. Next on the agenda is the blue-grey gnatcatchers' nest, a miniature, lichen-covered cup set in the fork of two sweet gum twigs. When leaves were just beginning to light pale-green fires on the trees, I spotted the pair at the onset of building. As the nest rose, they applied lichen-camouflage to its exterior with each new round of grasses.

Now leaves of darker green almost conceal the site. There's been a change here, too. Yesterday, I could see only the bill and long tail of the egg-warming adult. Today, the whole bird shows atop the nest: the eggs have begun to hatch, and the parent sits elevated on a pedestal of squirming chicks. I make the obligatory note and move on to the cardinals' nest, foundation of leathery oak leaves, lining of grass, that rests at the height of my waist in a grandiflora rose bush growing flush against a white, cinderblock house. The roses bloom sweet and pink, but the redbirds are nowhere to be seen, nor do I hear their hard-edged calls from any nearby tree. There's been an accident. One lightly speckled egg remains in the nest; another lies smashed on the ground.

When I was five, my father began giving me the names, sounds, and colors of birds. My mother read stories. One was *The Secret Garden,* Frances Hodgson Burnett's tale of the humanization of a mean-spirited, lonely little girl and the healing of a crippled boy, partly through the agency of Dickon, trusted by wild creatures—the Foxes that show him their cubs, the birds that Feed from his hand. When I became the mother of daughters, I gave them a Christmas copy of the book, and when they were grown, each with a daughter, I again read the book that had been left on my shelf, wrapped it a second time in festive red and green paper, and shipped it to the elder. On that last reading, a passage leaped from one enchanted page like prophecy:

And the secret garden bloomed and bloomed and every

morning revealed new miracles. In the robin's nest there were Eggs and the robin's mate sat upon them keeping them warm with her feathery little breast and careful wings. At first she was very nervous and the robin himself was indignantly watchful. Even Dickon did not go near the close-grown corner in those days, but waited until by the quiet working of some mysterious spell he seemed to have conveyed to the soul of the little pair that in the garden there was nothing which was not quite like themselves—nothing which did not understand the wonderfulness of what was happening to them—the immense, tender, terrible, heartbreaking beauty and solemnity of Eggs.

Thrilling not at all to prophecy but tugged by the compelling tumble of words in the last phrase, I copied the passage before I wrapped the book. It was as hidden from me then as a secret garden, as the contents of an Egg, that I'd be stalking beauty and solemnity in the trees, the fields, the thorny, chigger-infested brush of Great Neck Point. But the wonder, the heartbreak, and all the rest do not belong to the birds. They belong to people, to Aristotle, Pliny, Mrs. Burnett, and the keepers of nest-records. Not knowing what birds think and feel, nor what capacities they have for reason and emotion, we helplessly impute to them our human responses. At the cardinals' nest, yesterday's awe, today's slight clap of sorrow are strictly mine.

Yet, birds know something like heartbreak, something like grief. A pair of killdeer nested earlier this year on grass not fifteen feet from river's edge. The male made several shallow scrapes on the ground, some in a garden of lilies and volunteer dwarf marigolds, one on the well-mowed, well-traveled lawn.

67

The female chose the last one, lined it with pebbles and dried blades of grass, and began to lay. Easter eggs! Dyed a natural *café-au-lait* that bears dramatic scrawls of rich brown-red, killdeer eggs are larger than bantam eggs and look entirely too huge to be laid by a bird no bigger than a slender robin. If Aristotle's statement were true that the sex of chicks-to-be can be determined by the shape of an egg's narrow end, these killdeer eggs would invariably produce females, for the significant end of each and every egg is pointed; males, he says, emerge from rounded eggs. When the killdeer laid her second egg, we put a tomato cage around the nest to save it from the tramp of human feet. She completed a clutch of four, the usual number for her species. Thereafter, on my rounds with Sal, I'd see one killdeer on the nest while the other stood nearby, nor did they try to distract us from their wonderful business with the killdeer tactic of running swiftly elsewhere with a dragging wing. Early one morning, a day before the clutch was due to start hatching, both birds stood beside the tomato cage. The eggs were gone. The owners of the well-mowed lawn had heard the parents' cries at midnight, cries that continued loud and incessant till dawn. Cat? Snake? Raccoon?

Birds evince distress not just for vanished eggs but for fledglings lost. Three years ago, before I started jotting notes on record-cards, Eastern kingbirds nested high in one of our frontyard loblollies. The nest's location was unwittingly advertised by a streamer of Spanish moss, an epiphytic plant that scorns loblolly pines. Only wind could have put it there, or an architect with

a fondness for gingerbread trim. We watched the kingbirds through incubation of the eggs, through feeding
of the nestlings. The day the three young birds left that
rococo nest, we saw them hopping on the grass beneath the tree. Not quite ready for true flight, they
begged and received food from hard-working parents.
The morning after they fledged, I looked out the
kitchen window to see Sally digging furiously around a
crabpot beached on the bulkhead. The object of her
frenzy was one of the baby kingbirds, trapped inside
the wire of the pot. I released it and set it beneath the
nest-tree. At midday, it was still bouncing through the
grass and fluttering its insufficient wings; in early afternoon, it disappeared. Into the river? Into the belly of a
Great Neck cat? The parents wheeled overhead and
chittered for eight long hours till darkness at last stilled
their agitation and gave peace to our ears, if not our
hearts.

Instinctive distress at the disruption of a biologically
mandated act, intuitive recognition of chaos—grief
may not be the proper term for such, but what the
killdeer and the kingbirds expressed has grief's appearance and its ululations. In terms of a bird's short life,
sorrow seems to last as long as its human counterpart.
Wind-eggs, stolen eggs, eggs smashed or devoured—
from some eggs, no matter how beautiful or solemn,
nothing hatches but disaster.

And yet, mortal imagination has long been enamored of eggs and their close-held possibilities. It has
looked inside the windowed sugar eggs brought—laid,
for all a child knows—by the Easter rabbit, and it has

69

gazed with pleasure at the cottages, castles, and pastel fairylands snuggled embryonically inside. It has pitied the hapless Humpty Dumpty and wishfully, greedily dreamed of the goose that lays golden eggs. It has seen deity transformed to swan and treading Leda, earthly queen, who laid an egg with triple yolks: Castor, Pollux, Helen of Troy. Even in the early days, when many people knew full well that earth was flat, it envisioned the World-Egg contained in its own tough shell. I see that Egg now with the distant eye of an astronaut—mottled blue and brown, cupped in a cloud-lined nest, held beneath the deep, star-feathered breast of brooding space.

Eggs—while Sal chases rabbits or tries with great leaps to follow a squirrel up a tree, I see the real eggs cradled in the neat or sprawling, strong or flimsy, always functional nests at Great Neck Point. The standard twins fledge from the dim bower of MOURNING DOVE #.2 I cannot tell how many dove number one rears but see the incubating parent's body rise when shells beneath release their hungry contents. Long after the young have left this nest, the wind-egg sits in white abandon on its rim. The egg looks more defiant than bereft. Nor is it infertile. Slowly, snugly, it turns in the incubator of my thoughts. From such objects and events, the stories hatch.

How Paradise Is
Made Complete

≪≪≪≪≪≪≪≪≪≪≪≪≪≪≪≪≪≪≪≪≪≪≪≪≪≪

Sally moves forward in a steady, tightly controlled, slow-motion stalk that seems meant to make her invisible to the object of her attention. Her uncropped ears perk high. She stops in a point, neck extended, right foreleg lifted and tucked under her body. She stares intently at something in a damp rut on the pond road. I walk closer.

Snake. Tongue flickering, all else motionless, this one lies in the rut and stares back at dog, who has not despite her best efforts succeeded at her vanishing act. The snake's brown body wears black-and-red patterns. Hard to tell how long it is—sixteen inches perhaps if its curves were stretched into a straight line. Not poisonous: it lacks the vertical pupils and flat, wedge-shaped head of a copperhead or rattler. Northern water snake, that's what it is, likely a juvenile, for its colors are still bold. I call Sally off and head for the pond. Sal doesn't need to tangle with any species of water snake;

none are venomous, but all are aggressive and will definitely bite. Like this one, they don't confine themselves strictly to water but emerge on land to hunt frogs and toads. Our neighbor Dorothy has found a water snake in her garage. Another glides out in the evenings from its hidey-hole under our trailer.

Sal often finds snakes, many of which I'd not have seen without her, for snakes are masters of stillness, of melding their patterns into their surroundings. As with birds, I see them mostly when they move, the whip-like black racer disappearing into leaves and pine straw on the woods' floor, the rat snake that scooted, tail first, from the Carolina wren's nest in the shed when I disturbed it at its meal of eggs.

Snakes are a fact of life at Great Neck Point. The species of king snake that wears lacy white chains around its plump black body is seen everywhere—on the sandy beach at the creek, on our grassy lanes or the macadam of the road to town. Slender corn snakes, backs brightly decorated red-on-orange, bellies checkered black and white, sometimes crawl from the Point's fields to the verge of the dirt road. Manure-piles house worm snakes that look almost exactly like nightcrawlers. Eastern hog-nosed snakes prefer the weedy dirt near Mo's old barn; when Sal and I approach, they go belly-up and gape in a reptilian version of playing 'possum. Ribbon snakes, rough green snakes, and garter snakes make themselves at home on land, while mud snakes wriggle through the waters of creek and pond. In late spring, when carp tumble like fat puppies to mate in the shallows at creek mouth, the mud snakes swarm there by the dozens, swimming through the needlerushes at creek's bank. Their dark backs striped with orange-yellow imitate the play of light on rush-shadowed water. The snakes most at home on land also swim; rat snakes and king snakes sunning themselves near our bulkhead escape our presence by splashing into the river and writhing quickly toward another shore.

Venomous snakes live here, too—moccasins in pond and creek, timber rattlers in the brushpiles and high grass, copperheads anywhere on land. Sal hasn't yet found one of these. If she did she might seize it and give it a back-breaking shake, the fate of a garter snake she encountered on our fence-line path. One of the local mutts met a copperhead this spring and spent several weeks as a mighty sick pup, his muzzle inflated to twice its size, his eyes swollen nearly shut. Poisonous snakes are not the rule but the exception, their numbers amounting at most to five percent of the Point's lively population. But we all keep an eye out for them. A gunshot cracks on a summer afternoon: our sharp-shooting neighbor Lana has killed a rattler not five yards from her front door.

And once, not long before Sally's advent, I thought that I'd be a widow before I'd had much chance to be a grey-haired bride. The Chief, peaceably mowing the grass in the back yard, disturbed a timber rattler that had been going about its own peaceable affairs in the overgrown field bordering our lot. Snake emerged from weeds higher than a man's shoulders and made its sinuous way across new-cut grass. The Chief ran to the shed for a bush-axe. Returning from a walk in the woods, I saw the end of the encounter: arms raised, axe slicing down, and a thick dark rope leaping six feet into the air. The Chief had struck so hard decapitating the snake that he'd splintered the handle of the bush-axe. He buried the head in the woods under a foot of earth lest anyone step on fangs still capable of injecting venom. And when the black-banded gold body, stout as a man's arm, had ceased thrashing in the convulsive muscular contractions that follow death, we measured it: sixty-seven inches, including fourteen rattles and a button. Forget about the bite; a snake that big can break bones when it strikes. "It or me," the Chief said. "It had started to coil."

How inadequate we were. We did not use the body as we should have, eating the excellent meat and saving that black and gold skin at least for display. Rain started falling hard before the death-throes ended, and rain continued. Three sodden days later, we consigned spoiled meat and hide gone dull to a grave in the river. Only one small portion was not wasted—rattles and button, framed now and hanging on the living-room wall.

For a week after the bush-axing, the Chief trod the back yard cautiously looking for a second snake. Pliny, that Roman reporter of natural wonders, says that a snake is devoid of all feelings but one—monogamous affection for its mate, and if one of the pair is killed, the other seeks vengeance. It breaks through all barriers, travels any distance, and can single out the murderer in even the largest, most jostling crowd. Such unrelenting pursuit may be foiled only by putting a river between snake and self or by making the speediest of getaways. Like the avenging survivor, this legend, which is surely prehistoric, has broken through barriers of time, language, and scientific rationality. It has traveled immense distances, nor has an ocean hindered its journey in the slightest. Almost everyone at twentieth-century Great Neck Point subscribes with whole heart to the second-serpent theory. But though the Chief remained alert, he found no grief-stricken mate racing hell-bent toward him.

Prudence is the watchword. Stay clear of fields grown high with weeds. Don't cozy up to brushpiles. In sultriest summer, carry a light after dark, for snakes, denned against daytime heat, come out at night to look for their livings. The facile maxim "Black, turn your back" won't do to distinguish the many harmless snakes from the dangerous few; many a king snake or striped rat snake has perished by gun or club because it didn't look like something on which a back could be safely turned. And drivers go out of their way to run pickup wheels over any snake crossing our dirt lane or the blacktop to town. *"If you were not afraid, you would kill him!"* So D. H. Lawrence told himself in a poem about his encounter in Sicily with a snake, which he terms "one of the lords of life." The poem, otherwise eerie and splendid, goes peculiarly wrong with this statement. It is stark fright, not fearlessness, that beheads and shoots and mashes snakes.

Like almost everyone, I've known this fear and can sympathize with a visiting cousin, devout wife of a minister, who spotted the copperhead skin hanging decoratively in our kitchen. She clapped her hands over her young daughters' eyes and told them in a small, shaking voice, "It's a—*No-No!*" The Chief and I honored her revulsion by putting the skin away for visit's duration.

Horror seems the intrinsic response to any snake alive or dead; all primates, monkeys and apes as well as *Homo sapiens,* recoil with an aversion that may be genetically programmed. And people fortify instinct with reasons. Limbless yet agile and swift; their flicking tongues not truly tongues but organs of touch and, probably, chemical sensors as well; their never-blinking eyes impaling everything at which they gaze, snakes are so drastically unlike us that we not only draw back but impute to them an active malice. Snakes contradict some notion of rightness. Because they seem so manifestly wrong in the scheme of things, they allow us to persuade ourselves by some perverse and perfectly human reasoning that we are indeed upright in all ways—posture, thoughts, and deeds. Nor are they simply, inhumanly wrong; they are evil both in themselves and as the emissaries, the earthly apparitions, of some greater evil. We have always shuddered, then, in acknowledgment of their intimate connection with the dark side of divinity. That connection makes them sacred because all that is right and holy cannot exist except as the bright obverse of all that is execrated: blessing–and–cursing, life–and–death. Snakes, lurking under flowers, incarnate divine wrath and visibly proclaim it. They are weapons ever wielded by a deity to tempt and punish. Testament and myth and legend so insist, giving voice over and again to prehistoric fear.

Our cousin, a good and kind woman, would have done a more thorough housecleaning job than St. Patrick and scoured, shaken, broomed the snakes not from just one small island but from the world. She knows in the throbbing red core of her faith that once we listened to the sibilant offer of fruit, seized it, ate, and forfeited Eden. She knows, too, that Lucifer, the angel cast from heaven, can reappear anywhere on earth at any time in serpent-guise to whisper the same enticements. Satan—the very word contains an ominous hiss.

My classical imagination recalls the Greeks and how they saw snakes as instruments of heaven's vengeance. Goddess Hera sent two monstrous serpents to kill the baby Herakles, for he was lusty, squalling evidence of her husband Zeus' adultery. And Apollo, firmly on the Greek side in the Trojan War, dispatched a huge snake from the sea to strangle Laocoön and his sons, for Laocoön had tried to warn the Trojans of the treachery inside the wooden horse. And the head of the Gorgon Medusa was crowned with a glory of snakes. And Euripides tells us that the Furies, pursuing the matricide Orestes, used the snakes that were their fingers to clutch and hurl at him the "fruit of anguish"—a punishment—far worse than any he had known before. Yet, the Greeks also took a more benign view of serpents. They were kept as deity's familiars, fed wine, and cosseted in temples. The poet Pindar reports that

77

when the goddess Athena heard the dying shrieks of the snakes on Medusa's head, she took that fearful cacophony and braided it into a tune to be played on the double flute. Pindar also writes of an abandoned baby, the result of a god's dalliance with a mortal princess, whose life was saved by two grey-eyed snakes that nourished him with the "blameless venom"—the honey—of bees; the child, of course, grew up to be a hero. And snakes were scared to Asklepios, the divine healer, for they miraculously thwarted age by renewing their youth each time they shed their skins. Do physicians today think of Asklepios when they glance at the symbol of their profession? It is the god's staff, the caduceus, with two wings at the top and two ever-young serpents intertwined around its wooden rod.

But these are token nods, these Greek recognitions of the life-giving aspects of snakes. So deeply have theology and myth reinforced our built-in aversions that it's well nigh impossible for some people ever to see them as living creatures subject to the same natural laws that govern our human lives—feed, reproduce, and die. Yet, patterns and shapes can easily be learned to separate what is safe from what is dangerous or, like the Northern water snake, just plain ornery. The inclination of any serpent is to avoid trouble; it would rather go about its own snaky business than confront a large, nonedible member of another species.

Snakes have their well-known uses. Alive, they're given credit, albeit grudging, for eating rodents that would otherwise destroy crops. The king snake, immune to venom, preys on other snakes, including rattlers. Dead, they yield their decorative hides as bands for ten-gallon hats. Non-human creatures also find snakes to be handy providers. Raptors make meals of them. Titmice, blue grosbeaks, and great-crested flycatchers lay claim to cast-off skins and use them as foundations for the grasses of their nests. In our rural neighborhood, however, and likely elsewhere, the grosbeaks are rejecting snakeskins in favor of another discarded material that may be easier to come by— polyethylene bags and scraps of vinyl. The change testifies not to any decrease in the number of snakes, and a consequent shortage of skins, but to the ubiquity of trash.

On our walks, Sally knows the route and bounds ahead. I'm sure she often clears the way by giving snakes enough warning to slide into the shadows before I approach. Grass rustles and bends in a certain getaway fashion, or a tail-tip disappears into pine straw. A cause for regret: the sight of a snake has ceased to punch me in the stomach and raise prickles on the nape of my neck. Snakes have begun to look beautiful—the bold or subtle colors, the patterns that look like Navajo rugs or Roman mosaics, the dry smoothness of the scales in some species, the dry roughness in others, and always the powerful elegance of movement. Caution has somehow insinuated itself into the place once occupied by fear. I am not ready to touch live snakes and will never collect them except on a list of species seen. But I do most truly want the honor of observing them, of paying due respect to these lords of life. Paradise is not complete without its serpent.

Mallards

‹‹‹

Q*uack-wack-wack-wack.*

The Chief and I respond in kind. And here they come, three mallard drakes and one duck, paddling up-river like walkers out for a brisk evening stroll. These birds, however, have something more on their feather-brains than exercise. Not really tame, but not wild either, they're incorrigible beggars, cruising the shore-line squawking for handouts. Their route covers a good mile's worth of Cheerios, cornflakes, and stale bread, rabbit feed, dog kibble, and chunks of water-melon that week-end guests didn't quite polish off. Many of these panhandling excursions take place dur-ing the day, but the crew may also loom fully alert out of the darkness at an hour fit only for owls. I swear they know precisely when we've finished fishing the net at night. We move to the waterside cleaning table, and there they are, circling in tight, expectant formation. Sal at her post on the bulkhead lunges at them. They rear and splash, scatter briefly, and regroup. Nothing, not darkness nor dog nor pouring-down rain and a churning river, is going to deny them a feast of fish-guts. Darkness is, in fact, the better time for ducks to grab such bloody tidbits—no competition then from screaming, me-first gulls.

"You enjoyed last year's ducks so much that I thought you'd like more this year," Dale tells me. He lives away from the waterfront, near Mo's barn, and raised last year's group of *Anas platyrhynchos,* the broad-billed duck, in a backyard pen. He turned loose six females and a solitary drake. This year's "litter" was acquired from a friend in town. Dale says, "Every year he raises off a batch more or less as pets. He carries 'em around releasin' 'em in various creeks. So I got you some." Aha! The presence of mallards on the river is part of the solution to an overpopulation problem.

Throughout the year, the Point and the river furnish sets of markers for each turning season—the changing species of jellyfish, the shifts of color in grass and leaves, the stars making stately procession through the firmament. We could also construct a calendar according to the ducks. The mallard-months are those of high summer. Only rarely do we spot a truly wild spring-time mallard swimming amid otters and muskrats at the far end of the Courts Creek pond. The pond in April really belongs to the migrating dabblers—teal, wigeon, and gadwall, and in May it becomes the province of the little male wood ducks that cluster in their gaudy finery near the rush-lined sloughs at pond's

inland edge. At May's end, the females appear, de-
murely brown, with strings of fluffy ducklings that
zigzag after their mothers like ribbons on a kite's tail.
No later than early June, the last of the diving ducks
that winter on the river proper, the red-breasted mergansers, depart for their northern breeding grounds.
And we are left summer-long with the mallards. In
early fall, they'll discover the pond, the place in which
sensible dabble-ducks are supposed to graze amid
aquatic weeds, tipping tail-upward to forage as they
were designed to do. Just about the time that the mallards find the pond and start behaving a bit like wild
broadbills, the sky fills with skeins of sea ducks and
bay ducks arriving to settle in and bob away the frigid
months in large rafts on the river. The first harbingers
of winter are October's black scoters, the butterbills.
We hear the cries of the males, low and mournful as
the whistle of a distant train, before we see their big,
low-riding, black bodies and the bills that are heavily
slathered with a frosting of electric orange. With them
may swim one or two pairs of surf scoters, skunkheads,
a shellfishing species that dives and actually flies underwater to feed on the river's oysters. The bay ducks—
canvasbacks, redheads, and the bluebills or scaup—follow close on the scoters and raft communally a mile or
so out from shore. Near these rafts but never a part of
them, the small ruddy ducks paddle, holding stiff tails as
high in the air as stuck-up noses. Buffleheads, the bright
white males and their drab mates, claim the river close
to the shoreline, while hooded mergansers have the
winter pond all to themselves.

83

When the sun ticks toward vernal equinox, bay ducks and sea ducks answer the summons of increasing daylight and tune themselves to north on earth's magnetic field. They congregate, riding on the cold and foam-flecked waves in densely packed flocks. We look at these rafts, all of six or seven miles long and at least a mile wide, and see a concrete definition of that otherwise incalculable number *million*. Oldtimers say the rafts have shrunk nowadays, used to be ducks covered the river like a vast down quilt and drew a black veil over the sky. More ducks than I can really count still stage here for migration and, at the end of March, take flight. The rafts break apart like ice floes, losing a small chunk here, a larger one there. One morning, the river rolls empty. Except for a few laggards, the ducks are gone, winging their way toward the risks of summer, the chances of finding wetlands suitable for breeding in latitudes much affected by natural drought and drainage unnaturally wrought to create farmland where once there was marsh.

The migrators have already survived the earlier risks of fall and winter. Hunters are part of the duck-year's phenomena. At October's end, when the autumnal rafts are substantially gathered on water glistening as grey and oily as a polished gun barrel, the hunters flock in. 'Til early January, we watch their boats go out in the dim light just before sunrise. We hear their retrievers barking and the shots—tump! tump!—that signal each short day's beginning and its end.

Duck-fever rages hot enough to keep determination toasty warm on days of dripping noses, flesh turning blue, and wind jabbing icy needles into the deepest marrow. The shore becomes a stretched-out shanty-town of duck blinds. Several years ago, Dale erected one on pilings in the river just off Courts Creek. Over three winters, nor'easters demolished it board by board, but while it stood, it served not only as a better-than-nothing shelter for the gunners but as a year-round perch for gulls and a summer clubhouse for the local kids. A dilapidated blind used to stand in Courts Creek pond. Until Hurricane Gloria slapped it into the kingdom-come of pondside rushes, its weathered wooden ramp was a basking place favored by snapping turtles the size of soup tureens.

Duck-fever also heats a certain avidity to the flash point. Many gunners surely go about their duck-season business strictly for sport and food, with the latter aim on equal footing with the first. Their vessels are sober workboats, their black Labs well-trained, and the bag limits set by the Wildlife Commission observed most scrupulously. I suspect, though, that some who arm themselves aren't hunters but drugstore cowboys, wearing the right get-ups, talking the right talk, and totin' them weapons 'cause that's what real men s'posed to do. They remind me of the deer hunters I've seen roaring out of the woods with scope-bearing rifles and six-packs bungee-corded to their Honda 750's. During duck season last year, one trio of ducksmen cruised regularly back and forth past our bulkheads in the sea-going equivalent of a heavy-duty motorcycle—a white, eighteen-foot boat with an inboard-outboard motor and a fish-spotting seat that jutted on galvanized legs ten feet out of the cockpit. Dressed in yellow oilskins and a frozen grin, one of the threesome sat 'way up there riding shotgun. His legs were hooked around the seat's legs so that choppy water wouldn't buck him off. With such a rig, it's duck soup to bag a batch of sitting ducks. A boat like this is also suited for sneaking along the water's edge at night to moonlight deer.

Duck soup—we trade red drum, bluefish, and flounder for ducks legally taken on the wing. Nothing more fragrant and palate-pleasing on a cold, hungry evening than broth made of redhead simmered with rice and a garden of chopped vegetables; nothing better for belly and soul than teal braised with onions and celery in wine till it falls off the bone.

Quack-wack-wack-wack. The mendicant mallards coast our way again. The Chief says, "Hon, I can get you those quacks. Want 'em?"

It hasn't occurred to me to want them, not for culinary purposes at any rate. They cruise the river like proud and broad-beamed paddle boats. No heavy weather stops them; on days that gulls flying into the wind are held stationary against the sky, the ducks make steady way against the gustiest breeze and the most forceful current. They're not only seaworthy vessels but crew and passengers all in one—navvies, gamblers, freeloaders, layabouts, and handsome entertainers. After a fashion, they're friends. Besides, it's only the autumn equinox; the season on marsh ducks won't open for more than a month. The Chief does not hunt. He doesn't even own a gun. Nonetheless, I ask him just how he proposes to catch me these quacks.

"Easy," he says. "All I need is a string and some greasy fat." And he regales me with an account of his nine-year-old success in snaring a quartet of white farmyard Pekins. The method is classic for young 'uns who grow up in rural circumstances. Any kind of string will do, but the Chief chose that within handiest reach—brown tobacco-tying twine—and baited one end with a lump of hog fat. Then he went trolling, slowly pulling along the lure until a drake spotted what looked like food and swallowed it. Ducks, however, cannot digest fat, and anything that their stomachs reject passes with the speed of a bullet through their alimentary tracts. The fat, still attached to the twine, emerged promptly from the drake's nether end. As the Chief continued trolling, the bait was snapped up by another duck, and a third, and a fourth. Ducks in tow, he marched around the yard, but when that sport became tedious, as soon it did, he tied together the ends of the twine and let his captives pull one another this way and that in lurching, staggering, flapping, fall-down circles. Descended from mallards, Pekins are a pallid version of the ancestral stock; their feathers are bleached, and so are their voices. But the quartet began to complain loudly. Alerted, the Chief's mother made her complaint—with a belt applied to her errant son's backside. Only after their captor had suffered chastisement were the ducks unstitched. "Ducks before boy? Mom wasn't gonna give me *that* chance to get away."

I understand then that he never intended to fish for

87

the river-quacks. They've simply afforded him the opportunity to dabble in the pond of memory. He does shoot the ducks, however—ready, aim, click. We give the photographs to Dale.

Lord, love a duck. In times past, ducks were appropriately sacred to the lord of the waters, Poseidon. And they were thought to serve human purposes quite apart from those of cuisine. The Greeks believed that they could prophesy a turn in the weather: if ducks spread their wings and batted at the air, a strong wind was imminent. (It might behoove us at the Point to keep a weather-eye on the mallards; their prognostications might prove every bit as reliable as those offered nightly by the meteorologist on TV.) Then, one Latin writer credited the birds with healing properties and prescribed what may be the ultimate in quack nostrums: *Intestinum dolor sedatur visu nantium, et maxime anatis*—A griping in the gut is eased by the sight of swimming creatures, most especially a duck. Today, such helpful hints have flown out of fashion and memory, but some people do use the diminutive "duckling" as readily as did the Greeks to give a child or friend a verbal caress.

The river's mallards had not long outgrown ducklinghood when Dale set them free. The first time we saw this year's four paddling busily upriver, all were feathered in basic mottled brown. It took a month before the drakes revealed their gender, their heads taking on the iridescent sheen of dark green velvet, their black central tail feathers twirling like spit curls over their backs. All four were capable of flight when they ar-

rived to ornament the river, but they usually chose
webbed feet over wings as the favored method of locomotion. These days, when they're not sidling up to the
bulkheads intent on cramming their crops with kibble
or fish-guts, they go in for barnstorming. In a close
little squadron they execute aerial stunts and fly low,
buzzing the water and our lawns. Nor are they entirely
helpless when it comes to locating snacks if people
aren't around. They vacuum up the sea roaches that
scurry by the thousands on pilings and seawalls. With
the hyperactive efficiency of grackles uprooting newly
planted corn, they dive on grass seed sown to cover
bare spots in lawns. When they're sated, they hang
around on the piers like street-corner loafers strutting
and preening, or they settle on land near the bulkheads
and tuck heads under wings for a nap. Sal attempts
sneak attacks on the sleepers, but always they thwart
her by waking into instant flight before she comes
close enough to pounce. As far as the mallards are con-
cerned, everything's ducky.

It's not, of course. Last year's seven survived as a
team into November. By New Year's Day, only one of
them, a duck, still swam her rounds upriver and down.
A lone male bluebill kept her company. A week later,
she vanished. We'd like to believe that she and the six
trusting others responded to whatever wildness we'd
allowed them to retain, that they'd found their own
kind among the rafts, migrated in the spring, and
somewhere recreated themselves. It's far more likely
that the gunners did them in. Were they retrieved, their
leg-bands noticed, their kibble- and fish-gut-fattened

bodies served up and properly appreciated as a gourmet's treat? The septet's blessing may be that they covered the waterfront without the faintest inkling of finitude to ruffle their bird-brains.

This year's mallards dawdle nipping at sea roaches two piers downriver. We call them, "Quack-wack-wack." They put on speed and arrive in a matter of seconds. I greet them, casting dogfood on the water. *Ave atque vale*—this greeting is also a farewell.

The Trouble
with Ticks

⟨⟨⟨-⟨⟨⟨-⟨⟨⟨-⟨⟨⟨-⟨⟨⟨-⟨⟨⟨-⟨⟨⟨-⟨⟨⟨-⟨⟨⟨-⟨⟨⟨-⟨⟨⟨-⟨⟨⟨-⟨⟨⟨-⟨⟨⟨-⟨⟨⟨-⟨⟨⟨-⟨⟨⟨-⟨⟨⟨-

S al squeaks complaint. I cuss. Beleaguered, she
snaps at her rump. I swat my left ear. She scratches,
clawing away with a hind leg or nibbling at spots her
claws can't reach. I scratch, blatantly for exposed flesh
or with hand tucked discreetly in pocket to ease the
itches in unseemly places. The Point holds more pests
than Pandora's box. Ticks and chiggers in particular
are fond of dark, warm, tender crevices—the skin between the toes, the backs of knees, the undersides of
breasts, the armpits, and most especially the crotch.

Prowling Great Neck Point to look for eagles, eggs,
and everything else, I am given daily instruction, like it
or not, in creatures that chew and creatures with
fangs—the mandibulate and chelicerate arthropods, re-
spectively, not all of which have jaws or fangs, some
of which are quite beneficent and beautiful. The first
group, the chewers, includes insects, millipedes, cen-
tipedes, and crustaceans, such as shrimp and succulent

blue crabs. The second, the name of which, chelice-
rates, really means horny claws, embraces a motley as-
sortment—sea spiders, horseshoe crabs, tongueworms,
and a stunning array of arachnids. It's insects and
arachnids that present the most insistent lessons.
Painless entertainment or hands-on study that keeps
me digging deep—they offer both, and they're the
ones who set the curriculum. Prowling, I have little
choice.

Some lessons, not of the swat-and-scratch variety,
are given so unobtrusively that only later does the fact
of instruction sink in. Shiny-dark rhinoceros beetles
and their equally large relatives the eastern Hercules
beetles, grey-green with charcoal spots, lumber across
our yard. Luna moths, newly emerged from cocoons
hidden on the ground, climb, wrinkled and damp, up a
pine or sweet gum trunk and remain there like pale-
green patches of moonlight until their wings are dry
and strong. Swallowtail butterflies—tiger, black,
spicebush, and zebra—most often alert me to their
presence overhead by their shadows flitting at my feet
through the sunlit understory of the woods. In early
fall, fields bloom orange as monarch butterflies pause
in their odyssey to Central America. On warm days
after early summer rains, the moist lawns near the river
shimmer with the myriad wings of new-hatched skim-
mer dragonflies; the much bigger darners hover and
dart over the Courts Creek pond. Once, as I walked
the prickly pear path near pond's edge, I saw what
looked like a burlap potato sack tossed carelessly over a
lower branch of a live oak; it rippled in the breeze.

Closer inspection transformed this untoward piece of trash into a swarm of wild honeybees. By the time the Chief followed me to take his own look at such a wonder, the bees had gone. Other kinds of bees are more common at the Point: the carpenter bees that drill neat, dime-sized holes in decking and scrap lumber; the digger bees that make their solitary burrows in bare spots on the grassy lanes. Another local insect also dwells in a hole: ant-lion larvae—doodlebugs—lurk actively in the conical pits with which they've pockmarked the dirt floor of Mo's barn; treacherous as an avalanche or a California mudslide, the fine dust on the pits' precipitous sides tumbles downward at the slightest jarring and sweeps little, leg-waving prey inexorably into waiting sickle-jaws. Doodlebugs are among the insects that really fit their mandibulate name.

Mo's barn provides the easier lessons in arachnids, too. Everywhere, from ceiling to floor, spiders put on circuses in more rings than I can count: trapezes and tightropes, incredible balancing acts, stupendous climbs and lightning descents. One sheetweb weaver has spun a large web fine and sheer as a nylon stocking; it stretches from the mid-point of a wall down, down, down to an aluminum extension ladder propped on its side. The weaver is often perched at the lip of her retreat—one of the ladder's hollow rungs. Another kind of sheetweb spider lives and feasts aloft; it constructs a raveled, dust-collecting clump of a web along the undersides of the wide back-door's lintel, hides in crannies within the old wood, and comes like a rodeo star out of its chute to rope its prey in two seconds flat.

93

Outside the barn, argiope spiders snug their orbwebs eave to wall and exercise their ancient patience as they wait at each web's heart on a ladder of spun white lacing. Their name translates as "bright-face," but it's their bodies that dazzle, zigzags of gold on a stark black ground. Al's shed is also festooned in summer with as many as two dozen argiope webs; Bonnie forbids him to remove them because the tenants are quick to prize and eat the "bugs" she abhors. Other spinners work their circular artistry in the highest reaches of the trees. Beads of dew cling to silken strands and catch the early morning sunlight: it is as if the trees wear glittering diamond crowns. At a lower level, the crablike orb-weavers build spans across the prickly-pear path and the pond road. Shaped like their namesakes, wider than they are long, these spiders not half an inch across manage to bridge the pond road's five-yard width. They aren't shy; each places itself dead center in the middle of its elliptical orb. They look like easy prey for birds, but their white abdomens bristle with black spines. I try to duck under their space-defying constructions, the sticky webs and smooth anchor lines, but the nearly invisible filaments regularly boobytrap my upper lip and nose.

Most of the Point's spiders are objects of interest, not caution. Only a novice, however, would thrust a hand into a cinderblock or under an overturned boat without checking first to see if boat or block is occupied. Usually they are. The cobweb-weaving black widows take shelter in such cozy dimness. The Point also harbors the country's other spider venomous enough to injure humankind—the brown recluse, which sequesters itself indoors. I've seen widows a-plenty but never the recluse, depicted in guides as a small, drab-brown arachnid without any distinctive markings to alert the eye to danger. For safety, we count on the fact that it adheres to the general non-interference policy of every animal except the human sort, but I still shake out my shoes before I put them on.

I don't swear at spiders, though, nor swat them. I merely observe. Dangerously venomous or not, they possess obvious utility, devouring insects that plague us or being devoured in turn by other creatures in need of a meal. They've long served imagination as foes despised almost as universally as snakes, and they've been considered friends. When Robert the Bruce, fourteenth-century liberator and king of Scotland, was imprisoned, he made a companion of the spider in his cell. To judge by the entries that come my way in an annual writing contest for prisoners, the incarcerated still cherish spiders by feeding them captured flies and penning interminable rhyming couplets in their praise. The scientific name for their class, Arachnida, harks back to Greek myth. The princess Arachne wove a cloth so flawless that its perfection insulted Athena. Unable to brook being outdone at her own special craft, the goddess destroyed the cloth. In mortal fear of further divine retaliation, Arachne hanged herself. Not yet satisfied, the goddess turned the girl into a spider, the rope from which her body dangled into a web.

It's other members of the class Arachnida that warrant execration—the eight-legged stick-tights, the sneaky hitchhikers that mug their host, the wingless vampires that work their crevices—*my* crevices—by night and by day, the chiggers and remorseless ticks. What good are *they*?

The Point's latitude and mild climate, inviting to birds and marine life, also provide ideal conditions for a boggling number of insect and arachnid pests. Critters with two legs or four must be outnumbered a billion to one by critters with six legs or eight. Most of the pests that zero in on flesh are merely bothersome: the gnats that nip our ankles as we sit in the yard at dusk, the biting deerflies that swarm in from the hedgerows for precisely four weeks, mid-May to mid-June, and then disappear 'til the following spring. Sal brings in fleas, but we can eradicate these riders by applying a poison that enters her bloodstream and kills every flea that tries for a snack. And we can treat the sofa where she sleeps with chemicals and a natural agent, branches of the wax myrtles that grow abundantly in the front yard. Why myrtle works I don't know, nor can the toxicologists tell me, but tucked under the sofa, leaves and all, it keeps both dog and people from being liberally peppered by leaping fleas. As for mosquitoes, the Point's wetlands and puddles offer ample breeding grounds for several species, large and small. The largest, a veritable bomber with black-banded hindermost legs, breeds in wet lowland depressions and never travels far afield but sticks close to its natal stews. Though its habits fail to enchant, I delight in the rowdy bombast of its common name—shaggy-legged gallinipper. When gallinippers and their cousins descend in thirsty hordes, I receive my share of punctures but am probably more fortunate than most. Fifty-plus years of being pierced and feasted on have conferred an immunity, at least to the local needle-beaks; a bite no longer produces any welt or intolerable itch. Now, the most irritating aspect of mosquitoes is the low but utterly determined whine that accompanies each voracious visitation.

It took me only five years to develop another, though less complete, immunity. Innoculation began when my attention was fixed aloft on a nest in a pine tree and my feet were planted directly on top of a low hill of crumbled earth, home to a well-armed battalion of fire ants.

Their stings feel larger, hotter, more painful than might be expected of ants not much bigger than the pesky but harmless sugar-lovers that make busy, black trails across kitchen counters. *Saevissima,* the fire ants' species-name, labels them baldly for what they are— superlatively fierce. They infest the Point's fields and grassy lanes, yards and vegetable gardens. The sprawled or conical hills, made of finely sieved earth perforated by hundreds of small entrances, can rise overnight and reach nearly a foot in height. One large hill may hold as many as one hundred thousand workers that serve a single queen. A stick thrust down into a hill instantly summons the horde from its subterranean chambers. So does an incautious foot. In coldest weather, the ants are quiescent. In times of drought, they move sluggishly, but if there's been recent rain,

97

look out. Moisture gives them energy and brings them to the upper levels of their catacomb. Their homes invaded, they rally to defend themselves. Like spelunkers they descend into shoes, they scramble up legs like sailors climbing the rigging, and they latch onto any skin they can find, be it a tough callous on the foot or the tenderest flesh of an inner thigh. The formic acid injected by the bites leads initially to itchy, pinprick blisters and then to small sores that sometimes take weeks to heal because of tissue-death caused by the acid.

Of South American origin, these ants disembarked on U.S. soil in 1918 as stowaways on a cargo boat that made port in Mobile, Alabama. In the decades since, they've spread outward from that point like slow-smoldering fires traveling along a seam of coal, laterally at first into Florida and Texas, then northward. Not until the 1970s did their nomadic trains reach North Carolina. Now, fire ants have acquired an apparently unbreakable leasehold on the coastal portion of the state, and our most warlike efforts, our most ingenious remedies do not dislodge them from their encampments. Climate will thwart them in attempts to establish themselves much farther north, for they are creatures of sultry latitudes and perish where winters bring long-lasting cold.

Al and Bonnie have suffered their own sharp lessons in the ecology of fire ants: a colony can burgeon almost anywhere. Al discovered one small hill in the bed of his pickup truck; the ants had scooped up and ensconced themselves in soil and other detritus fallen from the logs, cinderblocks, and general outdoor junk that he had hauled in the course of a year. Earth and sand carried in by human vectors—Al's children blame his boots—were the source of construction materials for the hill Bonnie found in the living room beneath her sofa cushions. The vacuum cleaner proved a magic wand.

We battle fire ants. So does the state. Our county and a wedge of coastal counties south to the state border have been placed under quarantine to prevent the spread of infestation; such things as soil, potted plants, logs, and earthmoving equipment cannot legally be moved from our area to one that's unafflicted unless they've been officially certified as "pest-free." How many of us know about these restrictions is up for grabs. At ant-abundant Great Neck Point, the Chief and I may be the only two apprised of this arcane information. Meanwhile, we do what we can in our own bailiwick. The tactics run from walking around, not over, ant hills to injecting colonies with pesticides and pouring gasoline or sprinkling grits atop the earthen domes. Grits? Oh yes, I'm told, they eat it and it bloats 'em, they swell up and fall right out. The truth about offering fire ants this staple ingredient of a southern breakfast is an example of a simulacrum remaining after substance is gone. One of the earliest commercially prepared fire-ant baits consisted of a grits-like material impregnated with poison. The chemical has been forgotten, but the memory of grits has lingered on.

I don't condemn fire ants. Their obvious hills are easily avoided. They're a nuisance, all right, but they

99

don't damage crops, not even when they sneak into my bean patch and damage me, nor can they truly injure livestock. Sal certainly stands on their hills with impunity. The state's agricultural extension experts say that fire ants may even make an active contribution toward humanity's well-being by dining on assuredly destructive insects.

It's mites that drive my tongue to imprecations, my fingers to a digging frenzy. Before I latched onto the word *acarologist,* formed from Acarina—the scientific name for the order that embraces all mites, I asked the Chief what he supposed a specialist in ticks and chiggers might be called. Straight-faced, he said, "Exterminator."

Chiggers—red bugs in southern parlance—are far the easier to deal with. The adult form is visible on flesh as a rapidly moving red dot not much bigger than a period. It, however, is not responsible for the bites and the subsequent itch and the weeping blisters. Cloaked in invisibility by their microscopic size, the larvae are the culprits. They feast and run, and we're none the wiser until pustules arise as many as eight hours later. We have defenses, though. One is the knowledge that chiggers are creatures of the seasons: in cold weather, they lie low, mobility and appetite suppressed; in high summer, they range forth ravenous. We can also steer clear of their known hangouts— heaps of pine straw, rotting logs, and the woods, always the woods. But I can't stay out of the woods, not even in summer's sauna-weather that chiggers love. Repellents help, especially an all-over greasing with a product that contains one-hundred percent DEET. Local wisdom suggests some ameliorants I haven't tried—a flea-collar around each ankle, a slosh of kerosene upon the shoes and socks. The best remedy is a shower and a thorough lathering with soap immediately after emergence from woods. Needless to say, all clothing including sneakers goes pronto into the washing machine, for chiggers bivouac overnight in unlaundered seams and attack the next day. It's said with some authority that people can indeed gain immunity to chigger bites. The choice is mine, to stay home or wander, but every summer I surrender myself to the woods and my body to vaccination. Someday, this steady course of inoculations may take.

I have little hope when it comes to ticks. A murrain on their tribe! Pliny was right in calling them the nastiest and foulest creatures that exist. But, know thine enemy. On that premise, I've collected ticks from my every crevice, plastic-bagged them, and sent them off to the state university for identification. I've bombarded professors and agricultural-extension agents with questions. My veterinarian-daughter has also been dunned for information; she travels and speaks to regional animal health labs and farmers on how to keep tick-transmitted Lyme disease down to a dull roar among Wisconsin's dairy herds.

No, this part of my lessons in acarology does not concern itself with widely publicized Lyme disease, which also afflicts household pets. Something like fifteen percent of us—cows, cats, dogs, people—who are thoroughly bitten may become quite sick indeed; the rest of us develop antibodies. The deer tick, vector for the disease, has yet to appear in North Carolina, though it may well do so, most likely as a hidden passenger on Spot or Rover brought along on the family's vacation.

Year-round, as we walk through the woods, up the prickly-pear path, and home along the pond road, Sally and I are ambushed by ticks. They wait on the ground or on low-growing grasses; they lurk overhead on branches and leaves. It is our motion and our exhaled carbon dioxide that alert them to the presence of a bloodmeal. And here they come, mountaineers silently scaling our legs, guerrillas dropping out of nowhere to our shoulders. Two species find us delectable, the American dog tick, *Dermacentor variabilis,* and the lone star, *Amblyomma americanum.* The males of both species are brown and relatively plain; the females are gussied up, dog tick with a lacy white collar on her shield, lone star with a small white dot in the center of her dark brown back. I've asked the Chief, should I become mysteriously ill, to mention ticks to the attending physician; American dog ticks are the East's major carrier of Rocky Mountain spotted fever. Sal may be safer than I from being drained by ticks, for the systemic poison that knocks out her fleas also deals a *coup de grace* to acarids. She's patted often enough, anyhow, for us to find her few ticks before they try to engorge themselves. Sometimes, not often, I find my ticks when their eight scurrying legs tickle my thigh or neck. More frequently, they make their parasitic visits known by the itch that develops soon after they've penetrated and achieved adhesion. Several factors trigger the itch, among them the anti-clotting proteins in tick saliva and the cement with which they glue their sucking parts into the victim. And sometimes I know I've been feasted upon after the sated tick drops off; the sign is an inflammation the size of a silver dollar that surrounds a small, red, central pit. I think that Sal's ticks, scorning the taste of dog, occasionally migrate to me; the Chief vows that my ticks travel over the bed-sheets to his recumbent and unwary self. Except when it's still in the egg, there is no time in a tick's life that it does not require a bloodmeal. From six-legged larva (or seed tick) to eight-legged nymph, from each successively larger nymphal stage to full adulthood, and on then through mating and the laying of eggs, each growth-phase needs its rush of red. And each meal leaves behind its wounded flesh, its dreadful and unappeasable itch. When ticks indulge their sanguinary tastes, the males retain their youthful figures while the females swell. The nymphs, adult in appearance but not much larger than a pinhead in their early stages, can wreak as much havoc as the grown-ups. None of them, not dog tick nor lone star, recognizes a season; they are as avid in January as in July, and as swift to seek the most intimate lodging and board. In January, though, the clothing that keeps out the Carolina cold also makes me slightly less available to ticks.

In every season, I take protective measures when I venture into the woods—tucking pants into socks or wearing boots, smearing on repellent with special care given to snug places such as the waistband of my jeans and the legbands of my underpants. A homecoming shower helps, and prompt laundering of certainly inhabited clothes. And when I find the critters stuck fast, forthwith they are removed. The classic ploy to make a tick let go—application of a lighted match to the tick's back—has two results: blistered skin and a tick that's incinerated but still fully attached. The preferred method of extraction is a gentle but relentless backward tug so that intrusive mouthparts may be disengaged. If the mouthparts stay behind, they're treated as if they were a splinter and dug out with a sterilized needle. A splash of antiseptic speeds healing of the wound (though it does nothing to ameliorate the itch). Never is a plucked-off tick returned to the wilds; its fate is that of a convicted Salem witch—drowning or combustion.

If I were a rabbit, I might be better off. My vet-daughter says that cottontails and their ilk have been known to develop immunities to the ticks that prey on them. One of her colleagues says that people, too, may become less sensitive. But, like allergies that become increasingly severe with repeated exposure, my bites get larger, redder, altogether more excruciating with passing time.

What good are ticks? They seem the ultimate sorners, taking all and giving nothing in return except, perhaps, for infecting me with galloping mental acariasis, a horrid fascination with their kind. Yet, logic insists that they have a place in the food-web, a niche in the universal interlinkage of all life. A professional entomologist answers my query on the usefulness of ticks by informing me that two kinds of parasites prey on ticks and can kill them and that ticks are food for some beetles, ants, and birds. (My mind's eye immediately recalls *National Geographic* photos of the African tickbird probing for parasites atop a rhinoceros. Could we import such a bird to the Point and wear it like a pirate's parrot on our shoulders? Would we have to import a rhinoceros, too?) All right, ticks eat and are eaten. One of their functions on earth is catering to appetites, their own and those of others. Whether this is good or bad depends on who's the diner and who the dined-upon. Such a distinction, however, would never occur to a tick. I rephrase my question to the entomologist: What is the role of ticks? Where would *Homo sapiens* be without them? If they should find extinction overnight, how might our human machinations slip a cog?

"What is *your* role in the order of life?" the entomologist replies. "They have no role. Even God makes mistakes." We can manage quite adequately, thank you, without any ticks whatsoever, and ticks, tit for tat, can damn well do without us.

I begin then to investigate ticks in my own way, running to Pliny, Aristotle, and the lexicon. The designation for the order, Acarina, that they share with the chiggers comes from *akari,* a Greek word denoting a particular mite that infests the wax of honeycombs. The suborder for ticks is Ixodides, their superfamily Ixodoidea, and the family Ixodidae. The preliminary syllables, Ixod-, are derived from *ixos,* Greek for birdlime, and simply mean "sticky." Birdlime is a gummy substance made from the bark of holly and applied to twigs so that small birds, alighting, are glued fast by their feet and cannot lift off when the trapper's hand approaches. I try for a connection between ticks and this old-fangled method of ensnarement. (Four and twenty blackbirds baked in a pie. . . . Nowadays, does anyone salivate at the thought of small-bird flesh when larger—legal—birds are readily trapped in plastic at supermarket meat counters?) Ticks do stick to the source of their dinners as tightly as tiny feet to birdlime. But this connection, right or wrong, seems tentative and strained. Aristotle and Pliny make me no happier, though anyone can nod in vigorous assent to Pliny's disparagments—the nastiest and foulest creatures that exist. Both natural historians give ticks short shrift, and both believe that ticks arise through spontaneous generation in weeds or in the fur and wool of animals. For the fact of ticks, Aristotle blames sheep and goats and quackgrass, an invasive perennial that spreads its own obnoxious self in the manner of crabgrass. Pliny finds carthorses innocent of tick-engenderment but convicts oxen, sheep, goats, and most especially dogs, "in which all creatures breed." He also maintains that ticks have no opening through which they may excrete the indigestible portions of their meals and so, when gluttony has puffed them tight as juicy grapes, they burst.

Something's wrong here, and it's not the forgivable ignorance of early natural historians. Ticks, I am convinced, must serve some earthly purpose beyond their biologically programmed urges to feed and reproduce.

But something about them is fearfully wrong. In one sense they are truly mistakes, though I hesitate at indicting the deity for their existence. For all that bloodlust bloats ticks round and shiny, they are surrounded by an emptiness. It's Pliny, my ancient and frequently wrongheaded friend, who points me to an understanding of the nature of this void. He relates a charming, though mistaken, tale about the generation of caterpillars. He clearly and rightly recognizes many details of metamorphosis: lowly caterpillar to chrysalis to lovely and triumphant butterfly. But where does the caterpillar come from? Pliny says that at spring's beginning, dew settles on the leaves of radishes, condenses in the sun's heat, and shrinks to tiny, seedlike capsules from which minuscule worms develop. In three days, these worms become caterpillars. In this instance, it matters not a whit that Pliny misinforms. Imagination takes the utmost pleasure in associating dew with butterfly. It invests neither with harm nor guile but finds in both an endless supply of metaphor.

Butterflies have always engaged imagination in a marveling way. Granted, the order Lepidoptera—scaly wings—shelters some horrors: tomato hornworms and cabbage butterflies that chew the leaves of crops to airy lace, clothes moths that unravel weaving faster than Penelope ever could, gypsy moths that strip the summer forests bare as winter. But the idea of butterfly stands for all that is bright and beautiful, fragile, evanescent, frivolous, wistful, even sorrowful, yet perduring. The pictures in mind's eye range from the social flit-about to Lt. Pinkerton's abandoned lady.

107

Insects of many orders and some arachnids, too, even those acknowledged as a curse, have found habitats in literature, religion, and other realms of human contemplation. Egypt yields scarab beetles made of stone or glazed earthenware; they were used both decoratively and as symbols of resurrection. Aesop's fables are inhabited by insect-characters, perhaps most notably the industrious ant and the shiftless grasshopper. The busy bee dwells in cliché, while Jiminy Cricket acts as Pinocchio's conscience. Fleas—scowled upon, demeaned, but ever full of tireless nip and vigor—leap not only in proverbs and Aesop's tales, but in Shakespeare's plays, the opera by Mussorgsky, and poems by such as John Donne, William Blake, Alexander Pope, and William Butler Yeats. Even the cockroach has found a partisan in Don Marquis and transmigration as a poet, if a sadly altered one, to a New York newspaper office: Mehitabel the cat's friend Archy.

In one of his verses, using a spider as the symbol of the archetypal victim, Archy defends all who are cruelly, coldly swatted by life. He asks that we "pity the poor spider" and concludes with a resigned plea:

> I will admit that some
> of the insects do not lead
> noble lives but is every
> man s hand to be against them
> yours for less justice
> and more charity

As a brief for the poor, hungry, homeless, and disenfranchised members of almost any species, the lines make gruff sense. Spiders, however, can fend very well for themselves. And, as living solace in a lonely cell, as protagonist in an enduring myth, the spider has long been assured a safe place in human regard.

But who can squeeze out a droplet of charity for acarids? Who has thrown a net of fancy or devotion around them? Who has ever found a metaphor for humankind in ticks, or even the faintest sympathetic vibration? Not Greeks, not Romans, nor anyone else I've consulted. So far as I can discover, ticks figure not at all in myths and folk tales, poems or proverbs, nor in the visual and spiritual arts. They're stuck in one bloodless simile: tight as a tick. And, though tick is a four-letter word, no one's picked it up and hurled it forth as invective. It stands to reason that the little suckers have some use that human beings might recognize as good and just and worthy, even, of some minimal affection. Right now, however, there's trouble in the vicinity of Tickville.

But it's not the ticks' fault. It's ours—the particular way in which we uncharitably choose to ignore them. The trouble is that, while the little no-neck monsters gorge themselves, we've let imagination starve.

The Children
of Picus

ᘓᘓ-ᘓᘓ

*T*ock, *tock-tock*. A woodpecker drills for insects in one of the trees at woods' edge. I listen and locate the tree, a loblolly still wearing its bark, still sporting a few live green needles, but broken off forty feet up. It's less a tree than a stout pole for the support of trumpet vines, honeysuckle, and greenbriar. *Tock-tock*. I circle it cautiously, wishing neither to frighten the bird nor trip myself on a foot-snagging root. But there's no bird to be seen, though the tocking continues, slow and irregular. No food will escape this determined drilling specialist.

The bird is not a downy; its bill makes a daintier, less resonant sound as it invades a dead limb for sustenance. Nor is it a hairy, for Great Neck Point rarely glimpses this slightly larger cousin of the downy. Not a red-headed woodpecker; they're almost as scarce here as the hairies. Nor a sapsucker; this species only winters at the Point and drills serried ranks of holes in deciduous trees, not pines. A maple behind Mo's barn, the pecan tree in his side yard have been abundantly tapped. Flicker, pileated, red-belly—it must be one of these, *tock tock.*

The next morning, the same sound issues from the same tree. It is as if the sound is internal, as if the loblolly's dying heart has been revitalized, beating with arrhythmic strength. Look! 'Way up there! The sound comes from an echo chamber of a hole two feet below the tree's truncated top. The tocking ceases, and an acutely triangular, flame-tipped head pops from the cavity—the bird that some people at the Point call "cock of the woods," a pileated woodpecker whose red mustache marks him as a male. He quickly eyeballs his surroundings, emerges from the hole, and flies into deeper woods.

Dryocopus pileatus—the meanings of the names for his genus and species seem plain enough. *Dryocopus* translates straightforwardly as *Woodcutter,* a good Greek woodpecker-word used by Aristophanes in his romp through cloud-cuckooland, *The Birds.* Aristophanes and his countrymen had nothing to do, however, with the species designation. The scientists in charge of nomenclature dipped tens of centuries later into the bursting grab-bag of Classics and patched a Latin tag onto the Greek. Dictionaries and books on avifauna explain "pileated" as "having a crest covering the pileum." In Roman times, pileum (or pileus) referred to a close-fitting cap, but the word now survives solely as the technical term for the top of a bird's head. But every bird—every proto-bird, including the

112

pterodactyl—has possessed a pileum. If only crested birds are entitled to be called *pileatus,* then we might have not a tufted but a pileated titmouse, not a hooded but a pileated merganser. And how about a pileated pyrruloxia or jay or flycatcher? I'm sure that the no-menclaturists, looking at this particular Woodcutter, drew on something more than exact anatomical terminology to find its given name. Trained in an era that insisted on Classics as an inseparable part of any academic education, they saw not only the feathers thrusting skyward from the bird's crown like a bright flame; they also saw that ancient Roman cap. A head-hugging, conical cap made of felt, it was worn on holidays and given as well to newly manumitted slaves as an emblem of freedom. How red, how bold the cap of freedom flaunted by this bird that never was a slave.

He may have been a king. So goes a story from ancestral reaches of imagination, a story preserved in the names for the order and family of all woodpeckers throughout the world. Their order is Piciformes, their family Picidae—the Picus-shaped descendants of Picus. Some woodpeckers, the downy and hairy among them, make a third bow in the name of their genus— Picoides, or Picus-like. Sapsuckers, too, make triple acknowledgment: Piciformes Picidae Sphyrapicus, the last meaning "hammer of Picus." The name of Picus is reiterated with the insistence of a bill peck-peck-pecking at a grub-filled limb. Who was he?

A horseman skilled in training steeds used in war. A heartbreaker unremittingly, but always vainly, pursued by all the nymphs in his neighborhood. A lover

faithful to the one nymph he had chosen, Canens—
Singing—whose songs would set the trees and rocks to
dancing, gentle any savage animal, halt rivers in their
headlong flow, and make the birds pause in flight to
listen. A minor deity, son of Saturn, who was the god
of planting and the aboriginal king of Latium where
Rome would much later rise. And Picus himself ruled
Latium in his own right before he was twenty years
old. So says the Latin poet Ovid, who also tells the rest
of Picus' tale.

Hankering one day for boar-flesh, he put on a red
cloak fastened with a gold brooch, took up two spears
in his left hand, mounted his horse, and rode off to
hunt in the woods. And in those woods, Circe, the
same enchantress who had turned Odysseus' men to
swine, was collecting herbs with which to brew whatever mischief pleased her best. When she glanced up
and saw Picus, she developed her own hankering—lust
at first sight. Her hands involuntarily released the gathered herbs, and a fire flared throughout her body. But
before she could speak, making known her presence
and her desire, Picus had galloped past. A sorceress
blazing with lust is not so easily thwarted: Circe con-
jured the image of a boar and sent it across the hunts-
man's path. He followed, dismounting and tracking
this shadow-prey on foot when it entered dense undergrowth where, of course, Circe lay waiting. She issued
her seductive invitation. Pleading love for Canens,
Picus turned her down flat. But woe unto him who
trifles with the passions of a sorceress. Twice she
turned in the direction of sunset, twice toward the

114

place of dawn; three times she tapped him with her wand and three times chanted magic songs. He fled, astonished that he was running faster than ever he had run before—until he saw the wings that had sprouted from his shoulders. Outraged by this sudden transformation into bird, he hammered away, wounding oak trees with his hard bill. Red and yellow, his feathers took on the colors of his cloak and its golden brooch. And, says Ovid, nothing of his old self was left to Picus but his name. Canens grieved until she melted wholly into tears and evaporated in the summer air. As for Circe, she probably took up where she left off, irritably gathering an armload of malignant herbs with which to zap the next unwary candidate for swinedom or woodpeckerhood.

The shade of Picus may be enjoying the last laugh. Circe lingers scarcely noticed in a small corner of scientific nomenclature. Her name means hawk, and in its romanized, masculine spelling *Circus,* it now designates only the genus for the harriers. The children of Picus, however, form an entire order. Two hundred and four species of woodpecker, large and small, many of them wearing a patch of regal red or gold, hammer trees around the world.

Tock-tock, the racket of nest-excavation continues in the loblolly for a few more days and yields to silence, egg-laying, incubation. The pileated parents come and go stealthily, not advertising their movements with the usual raucous cackles. I know that the eggs have hatched when the adults begin bearing food to the nest. At the end of five weeks, two young birds, crowding

115

and jostling each other, peer from the cavity's entrance. They're fully feathered, though their bright red holiday-caps are not yet sleek but flutter in the breeze like frayed cloth. One soon vacates the nest. The other hangs half in, half out of the hole for two more days until it is brave—or hungry—enough to leave the only world it has known. But the departure of young from the nest signals no holiday, no freedom for the parents. Forced from the nest's security because they have simply grown too large for its cell-like confines, the young remain dependent. For the next two months, well into midsummer's heat, they follow their parents from tree trunk to tree trunk, food-source to food-source. The well-fed young are often larger than the adult birds; yet, they alight behind a parent and, imitating its catlike progress up a tree, beg insistently for tidbits, which are duly crammed into their wide-open bills. The Chief calls this urgent game "Woodpecker School."

The young pileateds are not the only birds that go to school after fledging. All atricial birds—those that hatch featherless and blind—depend on nurturing adults for periods of time that vary with the size of the species. We watch the feathered but still helpless young of other birds. A bumper crop of orchard orioles calls feed-me, feed-me from the hedgerows and deciduous trees. Newly fledged blue grosbeaks are herded by their elders from the exposed nesting site in the okra patch to the barbed-wire safety of greenbriars. Young pine warblers follow adults from tree to tree and telegraph their hunger in da–da–dit calls that sound like

116

Morse code. On the sandbar at creek mouth, the huge, brown-feathered babies of the laughing gulls lunge gaping at the bills of smaller, frazzled-looking parents. Sometimes a fish crow grabs the food in transit. Precocial birds, those like ducklings that emerge from their shells with down, bright eyes, and sturdy legs, also need guidance, if not intensive care, when they leave their nests.

Woodpecker School ends at the time that the wild cherries ripen on the tree in our back yard. The young pileateds swing on the fruit-laden branches along with other members of their family, the flickers and red-bellies. Their youth still shows in tattered crests and the amateur nature of their landings. They've learned to cackle as maniacally as any adult when they fly in toward the cherry tree, but half the time they overshoot the branch they're aiming for and somersault, crest over tail, before they latch onto a twig. And there, clinging to the slenderest stems, they dangle upside down and feast on every cherry they can reach. By fall, however, I can no longer distinguish this year's generation from its elders.

From secret egg to bold adult, an ancient transformation has again occurred. It's slower far than Circe's hidden, one-shot magic, but more enchanted, more ensorcelling because it is perennial and happening again, again before our eyes. If Picus isn't laughing, his Woodcutter-child flies undulating through the air and chortles for him.

117

Encounters with
the Gorgon

‹‹‹-‹‹‹-‹‹‹-‹‹‹-‹‹‹-‹‹‹-‹‹‹-‹‹‹-‹‹‹-‹‹‹-‹‹‹-‹‹‹-‹‹‹-‹‹‹-‹‹‹-‹‹‹-‹‹‹

We hear shrieks from the water. Soon, feet thunder up the steps to our deck, and ten-year-old K. D. pounds on our door, the nearest source of comfort. Her belly and inner thighs bear reddening marks that look as if she'd been lashed by a cat-o'-nine-tails. She's been stung by a sea nettle.

I hustle her inside, sponge off the angry, swelling welts with tap water, and pat her dry with a towel. Her eyes are still squinched shut, her teeth clenched. I reach for the jar of meat tenderizer and dust her as liberally as I would a slab of not-too-tender beef. "You're gonna live this time."

"Ah," she says and breaks into a buck-toothed grin.

People at the Point have as many remedies for jellyfish stings as they do for hiccups. Sprinkle baking soda over the afflicted skin, or—ouch!—rub on sand. Rinse the inflamed areas with ammoniated water. Pour on pickle juice or a dollop of engine oil. Use rubbing

119

alcohol or, lacking that, a slosh of wine (making sure, of course, that the wine is applied externally). Most people, however, swear by meat tenderizer, which acts in truly effective fashion to neutralize the acid of the stings. I prefer a quicker method—cool, fresh water followed by a terrycloth pat-down. But the tenderizer, not often used, sits perennially amid the herbs and spices near the stove because it's every bit as good as a band-aid to stanch the tears and unclench the teeth of a child who's not been badly hurt. Water soothes the physical pain; tenderizer does likewise and, more important, mends the wounded psyche.

Sometimes, as this time with K.D., the jellyfish pulse deep underwater. She bumped unaware into hidden tentacles that then released their burning venom. Sometimes, the jellies float near the surface, easy to see as they expand and contract their bells, arms and tentacles trailing behind. And sometimes they pile along the gill net's corkline thick as tumbleweeds drifted on a fence, or they wash up in quivering, translucent hordes on the sand near Courts Creek, where the sun's oven bakes them dry and they crumble into invisible powder. No matter what the species, the stage of jelly-life that we see is the free-swimming, tentacled medusa. From larval planula through stationary polyp to roaming ephyra, the jelly's infant and adolescent forms lack tentacles and, thus, all power to sting. Looking at K. D.'s welts, I think it entirely apt that the adult stage with its fanged and flowing hair was named for the most notorious of the three Gorgons. Pliny may have personally experienced the adult jelly's bite, for he mentions its burning itch. He also describes these free-swimmers as "fleshy leaves" and says they are nocturnal wanderers. Year-round they wander to the Point, but their movements are hardly restricted to the nighttime hours. The river clear in the morning can turn to jelly-soup by afternoon. The presence of jellies depends on water temperatures, salinity, the availability of food, and the push of a northerly wind to drive them upriver twelve miles and more from Pamlico Sound. Jellies do propel themselves weakly and locally by pulsing their bells, but in their long-distance movements, they are playthings of the winds and currents. And a rainy spring, sending freshets of run-off into the river, keeps jellies in the Sound, while drought, increasing the river's salt content, lures them to our neck of the water.

Like the changing guard of stars, like migrating birds and far-ranging fish, jellies also serve as markers for reading the year's cyclic clock. Late summer brings the nearly flat-domed moon jellies wearing a fringe of tentacles as short as a monk's tonsure. In early fall the mushroom caps arrive. *Rhopilema*—meaning "made of compacted water"—is their genus name. Their high, opaque bells have the resilient solidity of a rubber ball but, out of water, can break under their own weight. Lion's mane jellyfish, as tawny-gold and russet as their namesake, swarm this way in winter and breed or die according to the water's salinity; they are a salt-loving species. Early spring and warming water see the advent of *Nemopsis,* which has not yet found a nickname, though it might be called the tassel jelly for the way in

121

which its tentacles are grouped in four fat clusters on the rim of its balloon-like bell. And on the winds of late spring, when a dry spell has salted the water, two other markers of the season drift upriver and linger as the summer waxes ripe, then wanes toward autumn.

One is a comb jelly, not strictly a jellyfish, for it has no tentacles in its adult form and cannot ever sting, nor does it have the slightest power to propel itself. Like the jellyfish, it seems fashioned of compacted water, not fluid but not quite set, either, into definite form. It's the sea walnut, no bigger than the object that gives it one of its two common names. When sea walnuts arrive in force, we can rejoice and welcome them, for their presence in vast numbers indicates a paucity of sea nettles, a jellyfish that preys on them voraciously. And it is the transparent sea walnuts that lend swift brilliance to the sticky darkness of summer nights. Their other common name is phosphorus; disturbed, they flash pale green in the wake of a boat or tremble blue and gold on the corkline of a net that's being hauled ashore. Sometimes I find a near-relative in their midst—Beroë's comb jelly, usually more abundant in the colder months. The name serves as a memorial to an otherwise forgotten sea-nymph, daughter of the primordial, pre-Olympian god Okeanos, ruler of the ocean-stream that girds the world. (Some say, however, that Beroë was born to Aphrodite, goddess who rose from the foaming surf.) Shaped like small, clear bells that are striped delicately from top to bottom with eight slender, gold-brown canals (the "combs"), they look like errant ornaments from an underwater

122

jewel-box. I scoop both kinds of comb jellies from the river and put them back before the water can drain from my hand, for their fragile bodies flatten out of beauty and become dull in the unfriendly air.

The second marker of summer is the sea nettle, which comes in many colors. Some bear white embroidery on their bells; others are decked out in the dainty pinks of cake frosting, the purple-red of ripe grapes, the glow of a garnet, or dried blood's rusty brown. Rumor has it that only the red- and brown-tinted sea nettles sting and that their color is engendered by a successful feed. But color actually depends on gender and habitat. White and pink bespeak the males; females blush redder. Also, the darker shades characterize the adult sea nettle's oceanic variety with up to forty snakelike whips; fainter tints, the twenty-four-tentacled sort that prefers the less salty water of bays and estuaries. Winds and currents bring us every color in the sea nettle's rainbow.

And the sea nettle—*Chrysaora*, "with golden sword"—is the Gorgon of summer. Like the original Medusa, it can turn mortal flesh to stone. The severity of its sting is rated as high as that of the Portuguese man-o'-war, which is not just one organism but a colony sailing ocean waters like a pirate ship, with specialized components performing specific tasks. But the man-o'-war, terror of coastal bathers, thrives only in waters far saltier than those off Great Neck Point. Gold-sword is smaller, its tentacles trailing mere yards at most, rather than piratical tens of yards. The word *sword* should be plural, for each tentacle contains hundreds of nematocysts, capsules containing venom-coated darts that are triggered by a touch. Nematocysts retain their capacity for harm even after the nettle is dead. Though it's show-off safe to pluck up any jellyfish by its stingless dome, all that's needed to reactivate the nematocysts is a brush with wet flesh. Nor can the stings of nettles living or dead always be treated with fresh water and the handy-dandy band-aid magic of tenderizer. By a chemistry as cruel and selective as the anaphylactic shock into which some people go reeling after having been stung by a bee or wasp, a few who are nettle-stung suffer violent spasms of the chest muscles. Immediate massage may mean the difference between death or continuing breath. Luckily, most of us are not so turned to stone by the sea nettle's small-m medusa.

Aside from ringing in the seasons on the river's clock, what earthly good are jellyfish? They are carnivorous, using their dart-gun nematocysts to stun fish and shrimp, which are then pulled mouthward by the lappets—the lobes—on the jelly's bell. They prey, too, on the comb jellies, and the comb jellies are cannibals, eating their own kind as well as ingesting the plankton in the sea's rich broth. In turn, both jellyfish and comb jellies satisfy the appetites of other creatures. Sea turtles devour them as if they were popcorn. Young spider crabs and other crustaceans hitch rides and nibble out concavities on the tops of jelly-bells. Some small fish that are apparently immune to the stings weave amid the tentacles—butterfish and the silvery, four-inch harvestfish, near look-alikes to the angelfish of home

124

aquaria. They batten on their hosts' prey and sometimes on their hosts. People, too, eat jellyfish; in Japan
and other countries of the Far East, compacted water is
turned to a paste or dried and pulverized for human
consumption.

I feast on jellies in another way, pulling them in on
lappets of imagination. I think of aspic quivering on
my mother's salad plates, of fringed lampshades in my
grandfather's house. I see hot-air balloons, the baskets
gone but ropes a-flutter in the breeze. And the jellies
are fireflies winking not just gold but blue and green in
an underwater firmament. They are stained glass, miniature rose windows, in a salty cathedral; they are gems
on countless trays—opals and moonstones, tour-
malines, amethysts, and rust-red jasper. They are
winds and currents, and I the plaything drifting into
legends on their gentle push. Ocean's sea-nymph
daughter lives, old as the world, new as this morning,
and numberless as stars. She still breathes, still rides the
wandering currents as a myriad of fleshy leaves. And
the Gorgon still pulses; her hair streams tangled and
poisonous. Once again, Perseus defends himself against
her petrifying gaze by looking at her only in the polished mirror of his shield.

At the Point, we have no goddess-given shields for
our encounters with the Gorgon. And K.D., heading
breakneck for the water on a sultry day, will again offer her bare legs, bare arms, bare back, and tender belly
to the sea nettles. Again, I'll reach for the tenderizer.
But those of us who have aged into preferring comfort
to speed and appearance do have an excellent defense

125

against unlooked-for flagellation. The nettles have swarmed in overnight and, all right, the thermometer shows ninety-five degrees, with humidity sending the heat-index well over a hundred. It might be considered the time to dress down, to shuck off everything but shorts and the skimpiest of tops, to enter the water in bathing suit or birthday suit. But we dress up for water-work, be it fishing the net, innertubing upriver to the creek, or just plopping in to seek relief from heat. The only sensible garments are long-sleeved shirt, long pants, gloves, socks, and sneakers. Fabric of even the lightest weight serves to keep stings at bay. Clad more modestly than the most prudish of Victorian bathers, we plunge into jelly-thick waters.

The Swan
That Fathered the
Trojan War

≪≪-≪≪-≪≪-≪≪-≪≪-≪≪-≪≪-≪≪-≪≪-≪≪-≪≪-≪≪-≪≪-≪≪-≪≪-≪≪-≪≪-≪≪-≪≪-

"Hon, quick!" the Chief shouts. As I cook, he's been standing at the door to keep watch on the twilit river. I drop the stirring spoon and grab binoculars. Sal rushes outside with us.

A small column of large birds is flying downriver, white bodies luminescent against a lowering, late-September sky. Oh m'goodness, swans, tundra swans, migrating in the direction of Pamlico Sound, where sometimes they winter. We watch them till they're out of sight. Later, I sprawl on the sofa with Sally but cannot read the book that lies open on my lap. Swans! Tonight's swans wing through imagination, and so does a swan no mortal eyes have ever seen, the great bird that seduced Leda.

Most potent of the gods in the classical Greek pantheon, Zeus was given to frequent surges of lust for human women, and to claim them, he would often adopt a non-human form. For Io and Europa, he became a bull; for Danaë, mother of Perseus, who killed the snake-haired Medusa, he rained down as a shower of gold. But when Leda caught his fancy, he employed a ruse that would call forth not only his victim's sympathy but her ardent embrace. According to the playwright Euripides, she gladly folded protective arms around the great gleaming swan that fled to her in terror of a stooping eagle. The union of swan and woman produced several sorts of progeny.

One was Helen, hatched from an egg. And with her were born the events leading to the Trojan War. Another offspring was a hold on the poetic imagination of the Western world. "A sudden blow: the great wings beating still/Above the staggering girl, her thighs caressed/By the dark webs, her nape caught in his bill": so wrote William Butler Yeats in his renowned sonnet "Leda and the Swan." The German poet Rainer Maria Rilke, also in a sonnet, captured the god's amazement, his reverent awe, at the beauty—the very swan-ness— of the bird whose form he had assumed. But the myth and the poets, ancient and modern, don't tell enough.

Which swan? *Which* eagle? What species should take wing in the contemporary mind? What living birds did the Greeks of the centuries B.C. envision when they heard such tales? What birds actually soared over the grey mountains and green valleys of Greece or roosted in the trees of the sacred groves or plunged for fish into the wind- and light-hammered waters of the Aegean? In the poems and plays that I translate, the birds keep flashing by, calling, singing, teasing my curiosity as spring warblers dodging among high green leaves tease my searching eye.

128

Once the generic question was asked—what kind of bird?—the particular questions came flocking thick as blue jays mobbing a hawk. Which owl of all possible species was the one sacred to the goddess Athena? Which partridge to Aphrodite? A woodpecker mothered the god Pan, half goat and half man, but which woodpecker? Which doves cooed in oracular voices from the oak trees at Zeus' sanctuary in Dodona? Into what pelagic birds were the companions of Diomedes transformed as they attempted to sail homeward toward Greece from the smoke-blackened rubble of defeated Troy? And what carrion bird tore daily at the liver of Prometheus as he lay chained on the Caucasus Mountains as punishment for stealing fire from the gods and giving it to humankind?

The next question was, where are the answers? The search became almost as ardent and frustrating as my quest to add more species to the grand list for Great Neck Point. But my working vacations inside the centuries B.C. have led not only to close acquaintance with a handful of plays and poems but with several living—and lively—scholars who make Classics their full-time business. I consulted them. In turn, they told me whom to consult: one D'Arcy Thompson—"Englishman, wrote a book, oh, late nineteenth century, I think, but there's probably a reprint."

Next step, check *Books in Print* at the public library. D'Arcy Thompson is indeed listed, but as the author of a recently reissued book on Greek fishes. Back to the scholars I went, only to receive such responses as this: "If I had a copy of D'Arcy Thompson on birds, I would *not* let it out of my hands." It began to appear

129

that the book, the precise title of which I did not know, was itself *rara avis*. Giving the author's name and the general subject of the book, I wrote to several dealers who specialize in book-searches and out-of-print volumes. Only one came through with an affirmative reply but quoted a purse-breaking price. That single *yes* did, however, bring an important piece of information, the book's title: *A Glossary of Greek Birds*. It had taken ten months to learn that much.

Ten days later the book was in my hands, not from a dealer but from the interlibrary-loan system. Sweet Briar College released its copy, the author-revised 1936 edition of the 1895 original. While the dark red binding was still sound, the pages had become brittle with age; merely turning them broke off top and bottom corners.

But what a glorious book! The names of every bird mentioned in a millennium of Greek literature are listed in alpha-through-omega order, from *angulas* (a Byzantine Greek word for eagle) to *ōtos* (an eared or horned owl). Between, mythical birds like harpies, the halcyon, and the phoenix keep company with hawks and finches, chickens, storks, crows, and cranes. The pre-Linnean Greeks were far from precise in their terminology. Many bird-words refer generally to members of a family rather than to a single species. But D'Arcy Thompson was often able to make exact identifications. He combed the ancient writers—Latin, Egyptian, Hebrew, and Coptic, as well as Greek—for descriptions of appearance, nesting habits, flight patterns, and the like. He examined the visual evidence on

130

coins and gems, in hieroglyphics, wall and vase paint-
ings, and statuary. The entries are copiously illustrated
with reproductions of such art. To such far-reaching
detective work, this extraordinary ornithologist added
personal observations gained in a lifetime of studying
birds. And with the identifications, he included a trea-
sury of folklore—proverbs, fables, and accounts of
magical practices, some of them barbarous.

Sir D'Arcy, as he proved to be, wore this immense
learning lightly. His writing style is not that of the
pedant but that of the partisan who wants the world to
share his excitement. He was capable of wonder. In the
preface to the 1936 edition, he wrote thus of the shearwaters he'd somehow overlooked in 1895: "I did not
know how common these strange nocturnal birds were
in the Levant, nor how eerie, how uncanny, and how
notorious were their ghostly flight and wailing cry."
And, on the names of places and living creatures, he
said, "The merchant and the mariner brought strange
words home from overseas; and many a beast and bird
and hill and river had kept its pre-Hellenic name, hark-
ing back it might even be to the nameless and forgotten language which was spoken by the Gods."

A new question hatched: What kind of bird was this
remarkable D'Arcy Thompson?

The *Dictionary of National Biography* provides a
sketch. D'Arcy Wentworth Thompson was born in
Edinburgh, Scotland, in May, 1860. His father, of the
same name, taught Latin and Greek. His mother,
Fanny, died when he was born, and the child was entrusted to the care of an aunt at the home of his

131

mother's father, a veterinary surgeon. Classics and biology joined forces at an early stage in D'Arcy Thompson's long life. Educated in medicine and in the natural sciences, he spent most of his working years as a professor of natural history at the University of St. Andrews, Edinburgh. From the *Dictionary's* account of his career, he sounds like a man with the keen eye of an eagle and the incessant energy of a chickadee. He founded a museum that now exhibits his stellar collection of biological specimens from Arctic seas. His scientific journeys covered the world. He wrote prodigiously—papers on oceanography and zoology, a biology text that's still in use, and translations of such classical works as Aristotle's *History of Animals. The Glossary of Greek Birds,* 1895, was the young man's work; *A Glossary of Greek Fishes,* which surveys the waters as *Birds* surveys the land and air, appeared fifty years later. Laurels crowned D'Arcy Thompson from universities and learned societies all over the world—Europe, South Africa, India, the United States. He was knighted in 1937 and, the following year, awarded the gold medal of the Linnean Society. Ten years later, teaching to the very last, he died at the age of eighty-eight.

To the *Dictionary's* dry-bones account of the public man, a friend and a recent history of Australia add details. The history surprised me with the source of Sir D'Arcy's elegant moniker. His paternal grandfather was a shipmaster engaged in the transport of convicts to Australia. His son, Sir D'Arcy's father, was born at sea in 1829, on board the barque *Georgiana* as she lay off Van Diemen's Land. And on his son, the ship-master bestowed the names of a charming rogue who'd been transported two years earlier.

My friend, an eminent classicist who modestly calls himself a "student," gives the man flesh, blood, and breath: "My sister-in-law attended D'Arcy Thompson's lectures when she was studying medicine at St. Andrews, around 1938–40; she remembered that he would curse his biology students for not knowing classics and—as rumor had it—his classical students for not knowing biology."

The same friend acted as a consultant for my first venture into fifth-century Greece—a translation of Aeschylus' *Suppliants*. Almost at play's beginning, the Chorus of fugitive women sings the myth of Tereus:

> If a diviner of birdsong comes near,
>   a landsman who hears our heartfelt lamenting,
> he will think that he listens
>   to her who was Tereus' wife and now
> sings out heart's darkness,
> a hawk-hunted nightingale.
>
> Barred from her nest in the green leafrivers,
>   she trills a strange sweetness lamenting her exile,
> and the notes spill old tears with new
>   as she sings her son's doom:
> how he was killed, and she by her
> own hand's anger unmothered.

Here they are—Tereus, king of Daulis who became a hawk; Philomela, princess turned to a nightingale; Itys, Tereus' son who was murdered by his mother, cooked and served on a platter to his father, and resurrected as a pheasant by pitying gods. Here by implication are the other characters in the tale—Procne, Philomela's sister who was changed to a swallow, and Pandion, father of the two women, king of Athens, who now glides overhead on osprey-wings. (Some versions of the myth, like that of Aeschylus, reverse the sisters' transformations and make Philomela the mother of the doomed Itys.)

Exactly what birds are we supposed to see in mind's eye? A modern field guide to European birds supplements the *Glossary*.

The nightingale, *aēdōn* in classical Greek, is identified by D'Arcy Thompson as *Daulias luscinia,* a name that has been superseded by *Luscinia megarhynchos* but retains a magic because it refers to Daulis where Tereus reigned. (Nomenclature, like figures in Greek myth, undergoes amazing transformations.) The French term for nightingale to this day invokes Procne's sister— *rossignol philomèle.*

The swallow presents choices. The Greeks used their word *khelidōn* without exactness. It could mean house martin or sand martin as well as *Hirundo rustica,* the bird we know as the barn swallow. We can, however, legitimately imagine Procne as that familiar, deeply fork-tailed bird. It is Procne's children that build their mud-mortared, feather-lined nests every spring in barns and open garages and under the high deck of a river-neighbor's house. Her name is echoed in the nomenclature of the Hirudinidae today, sometimes with an Italian *g: Iridoprocne bicolor,* the tree swallow; *Progne subis,* the purple martin; *Ptyonoprogne rupestris,* the crag martin.

As for Tereus the hawk, nothing distinct can be envisioned. The legends call him *kirkos,* a poetic name for the sacred hawk of the god Apollo, a bird that Sir D'Arcy deems "not identifiable as a separate species." But an alternate version of the tale turns Tereus into another bird, one that imagination can both see and hear. In this version he is no fierce hunter, but, calling *pou pou pou*—Greek for *where*—he still seeks the sisters. He is *Upupa epops,* the hoopoe.

And many other birds once hidden in the dusty leaves of Classics now show themselves clear. *Glaux,* Athena's owl, still bears her name, *Athena noctua,* the little owl. *Perdix,* Aphrodite's sacred bird, is most likely the rock partridge, *Alectoris graeca* (literally, the fowl-like Greek bird). The woodpecker-mother of goat-footed Pan also keeps her ancient name *Iunx* (sometimes spelled *Jynx*) in modern nomenclature; she was a wryneck. The real wryneck was victim in classical times to a now-repugnant bit of magic; to charm back an errant lover, the person abandoned would bind a wryneck to a wheel and spin the poor bird dizzily around. *Peleiai,* the doves that burbled oracles for Zeus at Dodona, were better treated, though not so readily identified now. They may have been rock doves—city pigeons—or turtle doves; the priestesses who interpreted the cooing were themselves called "doves" or "dove-prophets," those "diviners of birdsong" of whom Aeschylus wrote. As for the companions of Diomedes, they became the birds of "ghostly flight and

135

wailing cry"—shearwaters. From ancient descriptions, D'Arcy Thompson was able to pinpoint the species: the great shearwater. Diomedes, an exceedingly minor figure in the Trojan adventure, might be utterly forgotten today if he had not been commemorated by the name given to another member of the Procellariidae—*Calonectis diomedea,* Cory's shearwater.

On the vulture that feasted daily on Prometheus, I draw a blank. The catch-all word given in literature is *aetos,* a non-specific word signifying some sort of eagle. The bird's behavior, however, indicates vulture. The report that Prometheus was chained to the Caucasus might nowadays be thought to limit identification to species that frequented those mountains rising between the Caspian and Black Seas. But lacking any ancient corroboration for such a notion, we cannot so narrow the possibilities. A Greek, hearing the tale, would most likely have envisioned whichever species was most familiar to him, just as he would have seen Procne as the swallow or martin that flew in graceful arabesques over his own gardens and creeks. Which vulture plagued Prometheus? Bearded, black, griffon, or the Egyptian vulture with white ruff and golden face? We'll never know.

Nor shall we know which eagle chased Zeus-the-swan into Leda's arms. The *Glossary* lists many possibilities for Greece; they include transients and winter residents, as well as permanent populations (now hard to find) of golden and imperial eagles.

But for *kyknos,* the swan whose form Zeus adopted, there are only two possibilities: the mute swan that

136

lives year-round in Greece or the whooping swan, a winter migrant. I choose the likelier bird, the one that would have caused Leda no startlement—the mute swan. Like Zeus, it is a permanent resident that breeds in Greece. And it is truly Olympian in beauty and behavior—the curving neck, the black-knobbed orange bill that could have gripped the nape of Leda's neck, the great white wings arching over its back, the I-shall-have-my-way posture, and the voice hissing the "nameless and forgotten language of the Gods," the singing of the wings as they beat away in triumphant flight. What bird other than the mute cob infused by deity was capable of fathering the Trojan War?

And the river's tundra swans—as they drew a glowing white line across the dark grey sky this evening, they seemed illuminated not by dying daylight but by some radiance burning at their very core.

Theophany at Woods' Edge

≪-≪

"*That* I don't do," says Betty. "All these men here, *they* can take care of it."

A four-point whitetail buck, suspended from a gambrel in the mysterious, dark green light of a grove of pines, is being gutted by the slight, bearded young man who made the kill. His single shot to the heart grazed and slit the deer's bulging stomach. Acorns rattle *pingety-pingety-ping* into the number-three washtub below. Carefully, the young man removes stomach and intestines. Just as carefully, he takes out liver and heart. If he were a Greek diviner, he would read these parts for anomalous configurations that might portend some future luck. As is, he puts the first two in the washtub and places the latter on a wooden table for later feeding to the hounds. The carcass, emptied of entrails, spins slowly clockwise, counterclockwise, and back again. Sunlight, spilling through crevices in the pine needles overhead, dapples the buck's hide with fawnlike spots.

⋆   ⋆   ⋆

Betty, my neighbor just downriver at the Point, doesn't dress out deer, though she can, if need be. She certainly hunts. Bright blue or burning cold, mid-October sets fire to the sumac leaves, starts to blow the sweet gums bare, and pulls the trigger on the gun-season for deer, a long season that shoots its final bullet just after New Year's Day. Well before the season begins, Betty has sighted in her gun. When the magical morning arrives, she dons long johns and corduroy jeans, a navy blue chamois shirt, old Herman boots shining with new oil, and the blaze-orange baseball cap bearing the black-lettered logo of her hunting club. She is its first and only female member. And she takes up her .243 rifle, a Savage with a 3x-9x variable scope. This year at summer's beginning, when I was up to my gizzard in gill net and fish guts, she invited me to tag along.

Her Bronco arrived in the yard at dark-thirty this morning. I piled in, lugging lunch and fruit-juice whistle-wetters in a small cooler, wearing my only weaponry—one of the Chief's cameras—around my neck. She'd given strict instructions throughout the last month. Dress in layers so that you can shed if the day warms up. Bathe the night before, not the morning of. Forget about perfume—deodorant, too—because you don't want the deer spooked by store-bought smells. She told me that some hunters strive their durndest to smell like four-legged animals; for a week or two before the season opens, they ripen themselves by avoiding all washing of bodies and deer-stalking clothes.

Some go to even greater lengths and smear their garments with home-concocted preparations of fortified hog grease that are supposed to eliminate the last residual trace of human scent. Betty has a word for such extreme measures: "Bullshit." In her opinion, based on more than four decades in autumn's fields, the fortunes of the hunt depend less on the invisibly persistent ooze of the human aroma than on the direction of the wind, the amplitude or paucity of the deer population, and just plain being in the right place at the right time. I'm dutifully layered and unwashed. I'm also wearing sturdy, lace-up boots that once belonged to Betty's younger son, a teen-ager who bean-sprouted out of them almost before they were scuffed.

At seven A.M. we reached the club's staging ground, a white frame ranchhouse set in a large, grassy yard hedged on all sides with thickety woods. The house lies about fifteen Bronco-miles from the river but only half a mile as the great blue heron flies. For its Monday-Wednesday-Saturday hunts, the club leases forested land on either side of the ranch from a timber company, and it also uses adjacent, heavily wooded gamelands administered by the state. Pickup trucks, some with dog-boxes for the deer-dogs, were pulling in as we arrived. Soon the yard contained a baker's dozen of hunters, whose orange hats and vests lit the grey dawn like a sailor-warning sunrise. A map was pulled out, and an aerial photograph of the leased lands. The decision was made: Today we hunt the gamelands.

141

A procession of vehicles pulled out, drove half a mile up the highway, and turned right onto the one-lane, graveled gamelands road. Recent rainwater still puddled in the drainage ditches on either side, and the loblollies just beyond the ditches wore wreaths of early morning mist. The hunters parked in a wide turn-around and walked down the road to take up stands five to eight hundred yards apart. I followed Betty— "Shhh, don't step on twigs," she whispered—and thought of tribal hunters going with bows and spears to steppe or savanna or riverside woods. Together they worked to find and bring home game. Today's rifles and shotguns come gleaming into the world out of factories, but the club's hunting strategy is tribal: team-work to maximize the chances for a kill. And like a tribe, these men and one woman will portion out among them any whitetail that is taken.

Chances for a deer are excellent this fall. Forage is abundant, its growth encouraged by two wet summers in a row. The deer have gained weight, grown larger overall—a hundred pounds where once there were eighty, and reproduced to the point of over-population, intense competition for food, and a general decline. Does are especially plentiful. In these parts, the doe-season will run for a full thirty-two days this year. On this first day for guns, when does are still forbidden game, hope rises high as a bound-ing buck.

Betty leads the way across a muddy ditch, points out the impression of a buck's hoof in wet earth, and motions me to stand beside a middle-sized loblolly.

Stillness. I lean against the tree trunk not knowing what to expect. Stillness, but not silence. My ears pick up the forest sounds to which they are most attuned: birdcalls—the *hweet* of towhees in the underbrush, the melancholy fluting of bluebirds in flight, a red-bellied woodpecker's *chark-chark,* the mousy squeaks of a brown-headed nuthatch. Beaded spiderwebs fill incredible spaces between the trees, webs that are three yards in diameter. Betty lifts a hand and cups her ear; she wants me to listen. What—oh yes! The dogs, Walker hounds most of them, have been released, and the pack is tearing through the woods, barking, baying, making more racket than ten lonesome boarding kennels put together. The day brightens. It's warming rapidly, and we start shedding layers. Betty grins suddenly. The hound-voices have risen in pitch, are whining like chainsaws. The dogs are on a scent. Betty lifts her rifle and aims down an alley in the trees, the kind of narrow path that a deer might take. Her arms are admirably steady as they hold that heavy gun. A shot, but it is not hers. From the stand just around a curve in the road from ours, the slight, bearded young man has taken his four-point buck. We mosey his way, the first to hear the telling of his tale—no dogs on this deer, the shot at thirty yards, it ran but left no trail of blood, fell soon thereafter, clean, clean, clean. His words sound casual, but gratitude and something close to reverent awe suffuse his voice and face. The telling is a ritual part of the hunt, a litany in autumn's book of prayer. Tale told, he touches the buck's ears—not as many ticks as you'd expect—and strokes its pale gold hide. His fingers stop at a lump in the deer's left shoul-

143

der; with a pocket knife, he digs out a healed-over shotgun pellet. This buck was a survivor of last fall's holy war.

"Who got that deer?" The question crackles over the CB radio in the young man's pickup. The dogs have ceased their hollering. We hear only random yelps. Several hunters leave their stands to see the kill. A boxy four-wheel-drive starts cruising up and down the gamelands road. The driver is the man whom fox-hunters might call master of the hounds; most of the dogs are his. Hunting deer with dogs is legal here—and necessary, say the stalkers, for the woods' heavy undergrowth prevents effective human penetration. The dogs hunt by instinct, not training, and the whelps run with the pack to learn from their elders. When a scent turns cold, the dogs, especially the pups, disperse, and some get outright lost or nailed by a car if they try to cross the highway. The job of the man in the four-wheel-drive is to round up the strays and laggards. A big part of this tribal enterprise seems to be the deer hunters' hunt for their deer-hunting dogs.

Betty and I follow the young man to the gambrel so that I may see how a deer is dressed out. Several club members watch as the buck is hoisted from the ground. One, who turns out to be the young man's father, says brightly, "Looks like that deer been eatin' raisins." It's new to me, this remark on the dark, round fecal pellets clustered at the animal's anus, but I recognize it instantly as a cliché integral to this communal rite.

144

★   ★   ★

After lunch the hunt returns to the gamelands and a side trail off the road staked out this morning. Betty parks at the intersection, and we walk the three-tenths of a mile to our stand. This area is swampy; cattails with shedding brown heads thrust up from the ditches. We stop beside a clump of tall dog fennel that bends over, almost touching trail's edge, under the weight of panicles in full bloom. The blossoms are tiny, white, and multitudinous, falling like spray from a dry water-fall, like a bride's lacy veil. We wait. The dog-pack has not given voice; the birds enjoy a siesta. October sun beats down on us as if it were July. Mosquitoes sing their avid songs around our ears. We've shed our layers till we're down to cotton shirts with sleeves rolled up. And we wait. Betty whispers, "Are you bored?" I shake my head. The body may be held in stasis, but the mind's speeding off in pursuit of its own game.

Betty has told me how she came to be a hunter. It was spun in her lifethread. As an only child, she had no chance to be anything else. "My dad was a hunter. He took me with him from the time I could walk." Her earliest memory is that of her two-year-old self accompanying him on a pheasant hunt. He shot a fine cock and allowed her the honor of carrying it home. She'd like to think that she bore the bird ten-derly, as if it were a ring upon the satin pillow of her small hands; the truth is, she dragged that rooster along by a leg. The wooded slopes and sagebrush hills of Washington state—these were the training grounds, where her father imparted sternly the no-nonsense rules for safety with firearms and, by some subtle osmosis, inculcated her with the arts of tracking, testing the air, and exercising infinite patience. She treats her gun with the respect due a deadly weapon and reiterates her father's rules as if they were the Ten Commandments. He died last spring. She is now his conduit, passing his instruction to her sons. She cannot, however, always translate what she does into verbal terms; much of her knowledge comes out of heart and bone and forty-plus years in the field. She gained admission to the hunting club through her husband, one of its founding members. The good old boys and the young ones minded their language and their manners, tiptoeing around her with the most polite dubiety till, soon after joining, the lady bagged a deer all by herself. I feel that her acceptance by the group has extended to me, today's rooster.

Women who hunt are not to be found in just any old woods, any old swamp. Those who do descend in spirit from a long, illustrious line that goes back to Olympus. In the Greek view of things, the deity entrusted with the care of wild places, wild animals, and the chase was female—Artemis, Apollo's sister, daughter of Leto and the head honcho, Zeus himself. According to the poet Kallimakhos, who tells the tale in a hymn he composed in the third century B.C., Artemis was all of three years old when she received her first bow and quiver of arrows and gathered her hounds for the first time:

146

two half-white dogs,
three with hanging ears,
one speckled (these could pull down lions,
    seize their throats, and
    drag them home still alive)
and seven Spartan bitches
    (swifter than wind in pursuing
    fawns and wide-eyed hare,
    keen on the scent of stag,
    porcupine, and the trace of gazelle).

This pack in full cry, she chased down five does large as stags, and each was antlered like a stag, and the antlers gleamed gold. She took four of the deer, threw gold bridles over their heads, and hitched them to her golden chariot as a trusty, goddess-worthy four-in-hand. The fifth deer was later captured bloodlessly by Herakles and delivered alive to the royal citadel at Mycenae. And women followed in Artemis' swift footsteps: bright-blonde Antikleia, who was chosen to be the goddess' hunting partner; Atalanta, whom the goddess taught to hunt boar with dogs and a true aim; deer-slaying Britomartis, who kenneled and ran Artemis' hounds and invented a net to be used in the hunt.

Legends accompany the hunt as closely and perpetually as the comment on "raisins." Great Neck Point has a story of its own, which does not have the stature of legend but certainly teeters on the brink of folklore. Nor does it involve a woman. It's about tall, lanky, broad-shouldered George. This is how I heard it from our neighbor Mo.

147

Seems that George got a hankering one crisp fall night to head for the woods and do him some serious moonlighting. He had no license, of course, and knew full well that, even if he were possessed of that official piece of paper, deer could be taken legally only in the daylit hours. But legal doesn't matter when a man gets clobbered by a hankering. Besides, the moonshine was working in him, as it often did. He picked up his twelve-gauge, stuffed shells and a mason jar in his pockets, and whistled to his big old, good old hound dog. Long in the tooth, a bit arthritic, and nose gone all to hell, dog was beyond his hunting days, but he'd be fine warm company on this chilly night. The two of them climbed into the cab of George's pickup, and off they rattled down a washboard logging road to a likely spot where George had recently seen deer crossing. The road was lined with loblollies that stood knee-deep in thicket. He pulled over, stopped, and stationed himself with good old dog in the pickup's rusty bed. He wouldn't need a spotlight tonight, not with the moon just two days short of the full and streaming so much brightness that he could almost count the separate needles on the pines. He rested his shotgun on the roof of the cab and took a sip from the mason jar. He was about to take another when—doggone, if there wasn't a deer, a spike buck, not thirty feet away at the edge of the woods. *Bam!* George fired. Clean shot. The deer dropped where it stood. Under good old dog's close supervision, he lugged that deer back to the pickup and heaved it aboard. And then, Lord have mercy, here came headlights blazing and bumping down that washboard road, game warden gonna get him for sure this time. Only one thing to do, and George did it. He tossed that deer over his shoulders and took to the woods. It wasn't an easy proposition. The trees turned off the moon, greenbriar grabbed at him, honeysuckle did its best to get a stranglehold, and deadfalls loomed up out of black nowhere to crack his shins. He heard the warden's truck stop, and a voice calling loudly. On he plunged through tangles and swamp and more tangles, and the deeper he went in the woods, the heavier that buck became. By the time he heard the truck start up and move out, the carcass must have weighed two hundred pounds, the biggest buck ever shot in Craven County. With the warden gone, George stopped his stumble-running and shed his hard-won prize on the ground. He nipped at the mason jar and turned to look at that trophy deer. Wasn't a buck after all. Wasn't a doe either. Damned if it didn't look just like that bad old dog.

The woods are about to give Betty and me a variant on this not-so-shaggy-dog story. I've been musing and watching grasshoppers on the springboard stems of the dog fennel. Betty grasps my arm and motions me to freeze. Something's crackling stealthily in deep thicket. She takes aim in the direction of the sound. Another crackle, another even closer, and a red and white hound with low-hanging ears slinks out of the woods. Her dugs droop; she's been nursing pups. Two more hounds join her, all looking woefully confused. Betty uses her normal speaking voice to say that the afternoon is just too damned hot for dogs to catch and hold a scent. I catch a scent, though—the scent of hound. The dogs are friendly, wagging, skilled at the.. deer-hunting task, but they stink. Their fragrance wrinkles the nose faster than a locker room packed with old sneakers. The hunters who try to disguise their humanity with hog grease would do much better to roll in the dirt of a pen holding beagles or Walker hounds.

That's it. With the apparition of heat-addled dogs, our hunt is over for the day. When we leave the gamelands, I think we're headed straight home to pull the boots off tired feet. We've stood and we've stood in two different stands at the woods' edge. But we're not bound home quite yet. The last part of today's ritual is still to come.

Betty stops at club headquarters, enters the ranch, and comes back laden with two full-to-bursting plastic breadbags—her share of the day's meat. A second member has also dispatched a four-point buck; the club's freezer groans, its belly filled. I remember something else that Kallimakhos told me: Artemis' brother Apollo often lugged home her kills. I'll bet he also dressed them for her. By all means, let willing men handle these little details.

Betty is forty-five now, five foot eight, and sturdily built. She wears her hair cut short in a greying helmet. Photosensitive lenses defend her eyes against sun and nearsightedness. In her soft, clear, slow-moving alto, she says, "What the hell, it was fun. I'll get my deer."

And she shall. Tomorrow she'll return to her job

in supply and inventory control at the Marine Corps
Air Station. By Christmas, however, a deer will
be hers. After all, she started hunting at the age of two,
a year sooner than Artemis took to the field with bow
and hounds. Granted, the goddess has been in business
for a long, immemorial time. But Betty has the advan-
tage of a whole year's headstart on the patron of the
hunt.

The Name of
Achilles

How brilliant, tonight's stars! The Chief and I sit near the riverbank, he on his cedar swing, I on a chaise. Sally lies by the bulkhead alert, keeping watch. Occasionally, she rises, points her nose at the moon-spangled water, and barks with defensive vigor before she circles and lies down again. By daylight we can often see what provokes her sense of territoriality— jellyfish, schooling fry, a water snake, the noisy mallards released by a neighbor, or simply an empty beer can bobbing downstream. Once, on a chilly March morning, the river barked at Sal. Hackles raised, she replied with full voice. When she paused for breath, the river barked again. No, not the river. Otter.

But tonight? We see nothing. She may be warning off a murmur of minnows or cussing the reflected light that ripples on the surface. She may be interjecting her own rude, third-party comments into the dialogue that land and river hold incessantly. They whisper tonight.

153

It may be that she's sniffing the air, using her nose to see things and creatures to which our human senses are blind and numb.

On the opposite bank of the salty Neuse, five miles away, unwinking security lights delineate the shore. Overhead, the Big Dipper ladles out a dazzlement of stars and stories. The sky glitters with lions and serpents, an eagle, a swan, a crow, a dolphin. Behind me, just over the tree line bordering the fields to the east, ancient tales reenact themselves in constellations. Perseus shows the edge of his silver round-shield as, over the half-dark horizon just out of sight, he slays the Gorgon Medusa. Almost in full view, Pegasus leaps squarely on triumphant wings from the Gorgon's beheaded corpse. A little closer to Polaris, Perseus' wife Andromeda reclines in languorous, unchained luxury. And closer still, her royal parents gleam, Cepheus and the treacherous Cassiopeia. You'll find the latter, say the star guides, by looking eastward from Polaris to a W-shaped constellation. Cassiopeia's condition, however, has nothing to do with the alphabet; she's as cramped as if she were caught in a crabpot. It's said that she broke faith with Perseus by arranging to have him killed the moment after he'd married Andromeda; to punish her, the god Poseidon caged her in a basket and hung it amid the stars. And there to this day she dangles rightside-up or upside-down, according to the season. In this case, attempted murder might seem to be outside the jurisdiction, or beneath the notice, of the ocean's lord, but Poseidon had an earlier score to settle. Cassiopeia had once bragged that both she and her

154

daughter were more beautiful by far than the divine, sea-dwelling Nereids, who certainly warranted Poseidon's jealous care.

I look at the wide and starstruck river and, at the edge of mind's vision, see mermaids. If legends wheel visible overhead, then surely they glide through the water, lie low on the sandy bottom, and play on the surface. And why not Nereids? They are the fifty daughters of shape-changing Nereus and a most abundantly fertile nymph; they are the fifty ladies-in-waiting for Achilles' mother, the sea-goddess Thetis. In the *Iliad,* Homer calls the roster of their names, among them Spray and Spindrift, Glitter and Calm, Power, Whirlpool, Speeder of Ships, and Never-Wrong. We watch—and watch for—their smiling or angry apparitions on the river, and often, from vernal equinox well into fall, we see their boon companions the dolphins.

In the scintillant darkness, a chorus from Euripides materializes on the river's broad proscenium and sings:

> Once the famed ships sailed eager toward Troy,
> oars beyond count impelling them onward
> escorted by Nereids dancing-and-singing,
> and dolphins drunk on the music of flutes
> leaped and dove splashing around and around
> the dark beaks of prows
> while hollow decks echoed the unresting strides
> of Achilles, Thetis' son. . . .

Fluent voices, wind instruments, the tympany of thunking oars, tails slapping water, and Achilles' restless, pacing feet—that's how it was and is again tonight. The Greek fleet stages and sets course for Troy. As mind's ear listens to the distant music, the swing in which the Chief sits creaks on its chains, the river talks to the shore, and Sal barks at who knows what.

In the company of Glitter and Calm, I stood on the bulkhead this morning to watch our neighbor Tom fish his flounder net—eight fine keepers and a mess of blue crabs. The bottlenosed dolphins had already assembled. Half a mile offshore, a large herd traveled in stately, determined file downriver to the sea and the waiting armada of ships—ships that can see where they're going, for eyes are painted underneath the beaked and bronze-clad prows. Suddenly, inshore, not twenty feet away—surprising fins! Two more dolphins broached the surface, showed the tarnished silver of their backs, and almost disappeared. In that spot the river is not more than three feet deep. We could see the great bodies circling tightly, setting transparent water into a clockwise swirl. Again the dolphins broached and sank and circled, ignoring Tom and me. These two were drunk before they heard the music of the flutes—inebriated joyfully on gulps of river-water that contained a finny, morning meal. They came close enough so that I could hear their exhalations, the "snoring" about which seamen told Aristotle. It's not a snore but the soft, abrupt *chew*! of a half-stifled sneeze. Then the dolphins turned, angling out in the river to rejoin the herd.

The bottlenose has swum the waters of the world

156

for sixty million years. Johnny-come-lately scientists have named it well—*Tursiops truncatus,* tower-face that's cut off short. The moniker aptly describes the steeply elevated forehead and the small, pug beak. Snub-nose—Pliny says this sobriquet is the bottlenoses' favorite nickname, one to which they'll answer with alacrity when called. He also commends them for the help they give fishermen by rounding up schools of mullet and driving the schools inshore where they may easily be netted. He cites as well numerous stories of dolphins falling in love with human boys and recounts what may be the aboriginal Greek tale of a human being rescued by a dolphin. Dolphins, it seems, respond besottedly not only to the flute but to the lyre. Once upon an archaic time, Homer's predecessor the master-singer Arion embarked on a voyage. When the ship stood far out to sea, the sailors plotted to kill him so they could steal the gold coins and ornaments he'd earned by his music. He persuaded them to let him play a valedictory tune upon his lyre. The notes rippling from the strings and the song on Arion's lips attracted a herd of dolphins. When he saw the great gathering, he leaped overboard. Immediately, one dolphin came, lifted him, and carried him gently to shore.

Less mythic rescues are attested. And dolphins do form teams that drive mullet and other schooling fish into the shallows for easy capture, but any help they give to fishermen is inadvertent, the result of their own urge to satisfy their bellies. As for falling in love, it's doubtful that bottlenoses become enamored of boys, though certainly something like friendship has been

157

seen to form between a person and this ocean-going mammal that may weigh more than a quarter of a ton. While the human being may legitimately be said to love the dolphin, the latter surely exercises only avid curiosity, a tolerant familiarity, and a sense of play. But Snub-nose? If I had acted on Pliny's advice and called out to the pair feeding inshore, if I had used his Greek word—*Simō!*—would they have paused?

I think not. Nothing would have kept them from making for the roadstead of Pamlico Sound where the flutes and the Nereids were waiting, and the deck of a beaked ship echoed under the untiring steps of swift Achilles.

Achilles once took on an alias. Before he ever put on a soldier's clanking garb and sailed for Troy, he wore for a short while the invisible armor of another name. I've stalked that wily name for twenty years.

Twenty centuries ago, the Roman emperor Tiberius challenged his court's learned men with several conundrums. Mythology obsessed Tiberius and drove him to what an ancient biographer has called "a ridiculous point of research." The questions he flung out seem taunts born of sheer pique at the failure of his favorite subject to deliver up all secrets on imperial command. Three hundred and fifty years ago, in his essay "Urne-Buriall," Sir Thomas Browne picked up two of the emperor's teasers. Sir Thomas' motive for repeating them was not, however, that of a frustrated mythophile. He saw the questions as minor and quite amenable to solution, if anyone wished to bother; his

own concern was with "a question beyond Anti-
quarism": Given our mortal state, what are the limits
of human knowledge? His answer, welling out of
bone-bred Christian faith, sets temporal human aspira-
tions against eternity, and it posits the practice of humility in this world as preparation for the next, for
"God hath assured resurrection." But in essay's last
chapter, just before Sir Thomas offers his reply to the
huge question, he mentions by contrast the petty que-
ries of the emperor: "What song the *Syrens* sang, or
what name *Achilles* assumed when he hid himself
among women, though puzzling Questions are not
beyond all conjecture." Sir Thomas did not waste time
on speculation but simply fielded Tiberius' riddles to
the present day. Both of them dangled like bait on the
end of a long, long line.

Why did I bite? Why not emulate Sir Thomas, who
refused such earthly lures? In part, of course, because
nibbling away at puzzles brings pleasure. In far greater
part, because the questions nourish wonder. Song or
hero, to name is to try for understanding, to recognize
singularity amid a bogglement of similar but not identical things.

A portion of the Sirens' song has long been available. Homer records the age-old lyrics, which human
ears heard the first time anyone launched a raft or
clung for dear life to a floating log. As for Achilles, all
I know is that it was not he who chose to cloister himself among women. He must have made rude protest
at the very suggestion, but his sea-goddess mother

159

could not be budged from a hard-headed determination to protect her flesh-and-blood son. Earlier, she'd tried to armor him with immortality by dunking him in the dark water of the river Styx, but the heel by which she'd held him remained dry, human, vulnerable. As a boy, he was placed in the care of the centaur Kheiron, and he learned to hunt and ride and handle weapons. At the age of six, he brought his first kill, a boar, home to the dank solemnity of the centaur's cave. He grew to be so swift that he could outrun his quarry, the lions and the deer. Later, as the Greek fleet assembled to sail to Asia Minor and ten years of war, it was prophesied that Achilles would either die young but glorybright on foreign soil or that he would stay home to lead a long, dim life. In perfectly understandable maternal fashion, Thetis sought grey longevity over the lightning flash of glory. It was she who dressed him—squirming and howling?—in women's robes and took him to a rural court. There he played her game both modestly and well until Odysseus, tracking a rumor of Achilles' whereabouts, came calling with gifts—distaffs for spinning, embroidered woolen cloaks, gold brooches, and a suit of armor. Achilles doomed himself to glory by choosing the last. His fame still coruscates.

Homer and other singers of tales proffer names that Achilles might have worn along with women's dress: Aïssa, Pyrrha, Kerkysera—Swift, Redhead, and Shuttle-Plyer. I think that the singers were fishing, trying to net something live in a sea of unknowing. They hauled up two names that describe physical attributes and one that refers to a traditional female occupation, weaving at a loom. They settled for lazy answers. I cannot believe them. The true name darts beneath the surface; it lies as hidden as a flounder on the sand, and just as one thinks it is caught, it flips away, slippery as an eel or a Nereid.

Meeting the ships in the Sound, escorting Achilles toward Troy, the Nereids—First Light, Queen of the Tides, Wave's Embrace, Harbor Girl, Welcome Home, and all the forty-five others—dance their songs and sing their perpetual dances in sportive, processional choir as they have since the world began. Music and movement—the theme is joy major, played *forte* in confident hope of gaining safe harbor. Joy shimmers fiftyfold on the water, flows warm in the depths; it splashes and booms, thunks ahead with the steady oars, rushes rich in foam along the gliding wooden hulls, and surges outward in a V-wave on their wakes. A gleeful energy invests the dance; the song rises loud and praiseful. And in the vanguard, the dolphins smile. The ships are alive, seeing their way full speed ahead through wide-open eyes.

Tonight, Achilles, when he stops his eager pacing, shall sleep most peacefully. Tomorrow, as the ships push eastward, accompanied by combers of music, he shall wake to stride the decks again. His mother might have named him Elpis—Hope.

Sweet dreams, Achilles. I'm also heading for my bunk.

No one wakes who answers to the Sirens' song, not sailor nor swimmer. Thanks to Homer, who records them in his *Odyssey,* there is no need to make conjecture on the words. In tuneless English prose, they sound like this:

Here, come here, much-praised Odysseus, great glory of the Greeks, so you may listen to our twinned voices when you've beached your ship. No one yet sailed by in a dark ship without listening to the voices issuing from our music-honeyed lips but he departed full of pleasure and knowing more than he'd known before. For we know everything that Greeks and Trojans toiled and suffered for on Troy's broad plain, and we know all that shall come to pass on life-nourishing earth.

In Homer's version, the lyrics are specific, but the Sirens' song may be sung to anyone. It begins with seduction and flattery, granting its prey the honor of being singled out by name and set above hoi polloi. The invitation bears no RSVP; acceptance is assumed, for no one has yet turned it down. What bliss, then, to listen and be assured that somewhere—here!—resides complete, compassionate understanding of every sorrow that one has suffered in the past. And what immeasurable ecstasy to hear the song's final promise—knowledge of the future! Riches? Fame? Requited love? Come, lend an ear, you'll soon find out. Don't let yourself notice the song's failure to mention the present.

Well, we already know what the future holds, though the present usually bids us forget it. Nor is there any need to puzzle out the title of this song, which is also its burden—*Thanatos,* Death, said in the ancient Greek way *t'HAHN-ah-toss,* replete with sighing and sibilance. The mysteries lie in the tune and its frightening beauty, its power to peel the wariness from otherwise sensible people as quickly as skin is stripped from an eel.

Water cloaks two-thirds of the earth's surface. No inch of it should not be marked with warnings like those on old-time mariners' charts—*Hic Sirenes,* Here be Sirens. Nor is the river free from infestation. Here, too, those large, soft birds with women's heads and the bodies of fattened hens roost and wait. Here, too, they whisper-sing their tireless lullabies to all who do not plug their ears or tie themselves with stout line to a mast. Too often, the Sirens make good on their promise of foreknowledge, and they feast on premature mortality, building their nests of human bones.

What triggers the song? What are its instruments? One evening late in spring the river shows us.

Our neighbor Bonnie shades her eyes against the westering sun and squints at the far shore. "What's going on over there?"

"Never seen so many sails at once," says her husband Al. "Not this time of day, at any rate."

Their daughter K.D. cries, "It's a race! Can we go?"

Her father shakes his head. "Sailboats don't race at night, and night's what it's gonna be purty soon. Plenty of workboats out there, too."

Dorothy and her husband walk into our yard. "What's happening?"

"Coast Guard cutter just came in. Something serious," the Chief says. "Get the binoculars, Hon." I'm on my way before he finishes asking.

The neighborhood gathers on our bulkhead to gaze at the far shore. Boats and more boats, like water striders on a pond, skim the water's surface and converge, clustering around some focal point. Small craft from the summer sailing camps bob beside full-grown ketches and yawls. A few cabin cruisers lord it over swarms of open motor boats. We see a little trawler that could be—hard to tell because of distance—the *My Way* or the *Wendy II* that both tend commercial crablines along our shore. And still more boats are coming, blowboats, stinkpots, a very large trawler making full speed upriver. Someone from our shore roars across, stern throwing up long roostertails of spray. The Coast Guard cutter, sleek and grey, idles at the heart of this activity. It *is* serious. The blue and red Search-and-Rescue helicopter from the Marine Corps Air Station arrives and hovers. Night comes; the constellations glitter in clear air like the jewels in a pirate's treasure hoard. The camps' boats have sailed home, but most of the craft remain, moving slowly over the water, their running lights like tiny, fallen stars.

Only when we turn on the eleven P.M. news for a weather forecast do we learn the reason for the fleet's gathering. A thirty-four-year-old man, out fishing with his wife in a rowboat, spotted a swimmer in trouble. Not pausing to take off his clothes and shoes, he dived overboard to help her. The teenaged swimmer, rescued by someone else, is reported in stable condition at the hospital. The man has disappeared. The boats make search.

164

The day has been a model of the kind that fore-casters call "perfect"—a balmy, blue, come-hither day, exactly right for playing hookey and heading for the beach, for letting a fishing rod take precedence over work. The water, too, was perfect, surface only lightly ruffled by a southwesterly breeze and the deeper chill baked out by a sun approaching summer solstice. As the man and his wife fished, the girl splashed with her friends in the shallows over a sandbar. And she stepped off the bar into water over her head. The sheriff said later, "You wade out and after you wade out, you forget where the sandbar is. It's dangerous waters." The sandbar drops off steeply into a fifteen-foot hole that's swept by a strong current.

News the next day brings word from the river's western shore that the swimmer will make full recovery and that her would-be rescuer has been found. The large trawler that we saw making speedy way upriver belongs to the man's father, a commercial fisherman. His crew lowered the nets and pulled the river for thirty minutes until they brought up the body of the son, still clad in shoes, blue pants, and yellow shirt.

That time the Sirens were cheated of bones and a soft, damp, blue and yellow lining for their nest.

Until that night and the mournful day after, I would have guessed that their song might be triggered by a cloudburst or a gale, in one of the howling nor'easters that strike the river suddenly and tear small craft from their skippers' control. The guess would have been off course by one hundred and eighty degrees. The Sirens croon only on the fairest days and nights, not in foul

165

weather. Not long ago they were heard by the boy who decided to sleep away a sultry night in his moored skiff, as he'd done many times with impunity; at daybreak, the boat was found overturned. And every year, sure as the river flows to the sea, the song will be issued and answered.

Perhaps Tiberius, a stormy man, overlooked the most obvious clues to this puzzle. Homer does not name the Sirens, who in his reckoning numbered only two—those "twinned voices." Some later classical poets, however, recognized a bevy and showed keen knowledge of the Sirens' nature in the names they listed: Virgin-Face, Shining Face, Face That Casts Spells, Clear Voice and Limpid, Voice That Sparkles and Voice That Bewitches, Dancing-and-Singing, Persuader, Pain-Lifter, and Perfect Fulfillment. Fair-weather names: they gleam and offer every enticement.

Today, as they always have, the Sirens capitalize on their fatal loveliness, nor is their crooning any less seductive than it was for long-drowned mariners. The river provides as many tunes as there are sunny days. Look! The sky's immaculate, no clouds at all. Sun beams down on translucent sea; the light springs back toward heaven. A breath of wind tickles the water into motion as gentle as the rocking of a baby in its mother's arms. Listen! Climbing the sand, falling back, the wavelets fizz like palest sparkling wine. The day will be azure and hot, the water cool, a respite from the onerous demands of intellect and earning a buck. This is no time to toil indoors. And the instant that chronic occupations are shrugged off, even before the beach towels and the tackle box are packed, the song begins. Its barely audible melody may be overridden by a portable radio blaring out rock or country-and-western. *Pianissimo,* the tune winds out nonetheless: the susurrous rise and lapse of tiny waves, light striking the water with a honeyed crash, the beat-beat-beat of an expectant heart. Plucked by desire, lulled to forgetfulness of peril, its victims are the instruments, the gut-strung lyres and flutes made of bone, on which the song is played. We know how it ends and ought to keep in mind that the song has been around for millennia. By popular request, it will be played again.

One of Tiberius' questions has found an answer. It tolls through time like a death knell and might have given him pause in his fury. But the name of Achilles? I am as baffled as the emperor.

"The certainty of death," says Sir Thomas, "is attended by uncertainties, in time, manner, places." Achilles will not ever hear the Sirens, will not come close to hearing them. But, as Nereids and dolphins guide him toward Troy, he is certainly aware of the last trick that his future holds and knew about it the moment he flung off his woman's clothes and name to take up armor. He even knows the manner of his dying—that vulnerable heel—if not the place and the hour. It is still concealed from him, too, that he shall cause the war to drag on for nearly ten years because he'll sulk in his tent refusing to fight. It is also hidden that he'll lend the armor Odysseus gave him to his cousin and best friend, who shall fight in Achilles'

167

stead and be slaughtered. In a rage of grief, Achilles shall stalk forth. The Nereids will bring him new armor ordered by his goddess-mother and forged by Hephaistos, the heavenly smith—armor made of living gold. And when such armor is laid before him, Achilles shall hold his breath, but just for an instant. Then, all business, he'll strap on the divinely forged breastplate and greaves, place on his head the Olympian helmet, lift up the heavy, numinous shield, and stride forth to fight. He shall kill the prince Hector, first and last hope of the Trojans. At war's end he, too, shall die without returning to Greek soil.

How did Achilles take to sequestration in the women's quarters? It couldn't have been easy. Unexercised legs must have ached to outrun lions and deer, and his body, used to supple leather clothing, must have itched intolerably in its cocoon of scratchy woollen robes. Amid feminine tidiness—no cobwebs, no thick soot from cooking fires—he must have been homesick for the not-too-clean but friendly fustiness of Kheiron's cave. He must have waited quivering like a trapped animal and hoping for better things.

I am almost willing to settle for Hope, except it seems a name his goddess-mother would have chosen; it expresses her desire, not his. Surely, the youthful Achilles struck some bargain with her before he acceded to her wishes and sat himself down at a loom in the women's quarters of a hayseed court. Surely, he reserved the right to select the name by which his giggling, preening, innocent companions would know him, a name that would speak out loud some quality he found within himself. Fortitude? Dare-All? Excellence? Honor? Maybe he claimed his ultimate goal, Glory. Perhaps he chose to describe his condition, Gift of the Goddess. Maybe he joked—Crafty, Man-Battler, or Impregnable. He might have named himself Patience so that calling voices would remind him constantly of the virtue he most desperately needed to exercise.

I am not satisfied.

October night four years ago: as Orion hunts in white silence overhead, the Chief brings a fish just pulled from the net to our granddaughter Melissa.

"What's 'at?" she says. "What name?"

"Croaker," he replies. Obligingly, it vibrates its gas bladder to make the sound for which it's called—a rapid, guttural series of burps. Small girl is satisfied until the next fish comes in.

She's only three. I've tried to put her to bed, but she's resisted sleep because our neighbor Tom's yard bustles and roars with the excitement of hauling in gill nets. Floodlights blaze. People talk and laugh as they extract fish from the meshes. Knives and scalers clatter on the cleaning table. Dogs bark. Sally grabs a menhaden dropped on the grass and crunches on its head; she'll bury the rest like a bone. Earlier, I ceased resisting Melissa's resistance, wrapped her in an afghan, carried her to Tom's yard, and plopped her in a lawn chaise. There she reclines imperiously, her long blonde hair shining like palest honey in the floodlight's beam. Her gaze tonight is glassy, half-lidded. She should be worn out, but she demands the name of every fish she sees. She doesn't miss many.

Menhaden, mullet, shad, more croaker—the roll call is repetitive, monotonous. The Chief and I inject variety by using local names—fatback and yellowfin and pogie for menhaden, nanny for gizzard shad. Someone brings over a slender brown fish that looks like a foot-long tube of pepperoni—an inshore lizardfish.

"Name!"

Formally, this species of lizardfish is *Synodus foetens.* I translate the latter term. "This one's a stinker."

She giggles. Soon she does not wait for us to make the introductions but becomes a small, inspired, female version of Adam, touching everything we bring and naming it before we can open our mouths. I am amazed at the consistency with which she applies the epithets that she invents.

"Sharptop!" Pinfish.

"Greeny!" Bluefish. Yes, she's right; its upper sides reflect a green-gold light.

"Stripey!" A streamlined, black-and-silver jumping mullet, long enough in the net to have lost its jump. "Flappy stripe!" A mullet that's doing its damnedest to flip from the Chief's hand.

When she's presented with a sea robin, she knows instantly what it is: "Sparkle blue eyes!" On a cold October night, a hint of the tropics: the sea robin's eyes are the electric turquoise of shoaling Caribbean waters. Small girl wants to keep it, take it to her bed as if it were a toy. But it's quite alive. We give it back to the river. Her fancy is soon enough occupied by a "Yuckfish," a shad that's been gutted by an eel. Though the child is half-pint drunk on tiredness and starts to slur her words, she does not cease the naming game until the last fish is pulled from the last net. When the Chief picks her up to carry her home, she finally closes her own sea-robin eyes.

Melissa has been catching the fish in a net of names. Too young to grasp the import of her act, she has controlled not the critters but her perceptions of them. Instinctively, with great delight, she has created for herself some tiny order out of chaos. I ought to take her along on my own quest.

Melissa—would that have been Achilles' pseudonym? Ancient and Greek, it means Honeybee. Achilles would have known the word and could have used it to describe himself in two ways. One concentrates on sweetness: according to several classical reporters, his hair was not flaming red but golden, perhaps the sunny gold of pollen or the deep red-gold of basswood honey. The Greeks had a powerful sweet tooth; honey satisfied their tongues and their imaginations, oozing not just from the comb but from countless compound adjectives, such as "music-honeyed" for the Sirens' lips. The other way in which Honeybee might have described him puts emphasis on the sting. What torment for his buzzing adolescent hormones that he was hived in a garden of country flowers. Old rumor has it that he did unsheathe his weapon in the women's quarters and left behind at least one swelling, his son, Neoptolemos.

171

Melissa? No. Despite its hidden sting, it is too slow and cloying for a restless man.

The name comes unexpectedly. The river brings it in a box.

All day, the wind has blown steady and hard out of the southeast, not its usual quarter. At dawn, a froth of whitecaps five miles wide surged downstream, and rain came pelting in horizontal, wind-flung sheets. An hour later, calm: the weather held its harsh breath long enough for us to wade the gill nets and bring in flounder, croaker, spot, and four nice puppy drum. Then, the tempest revved up again. Just after lunch, the radio announced a tornado watch effective till sundown. By late afternoon, the river-version of a twister—a waterspout—looked quite possible. The flurries of rain had stopped, but the winds blasted out of the grey southeast harder than ever.

And after supper? Tornado watch be damned. Almost no one has stayed indoors. Most of the people on our patch of shore are out walking the riverbed. The general posture, however, is hardly that of casual strollers. Leaning at sixty-degree angles, we force our way against the wind or, hands on knees, eyes on the sand, we're mobile but bent at the waist like upside-down J-hooks. Dorothy, Al, a passel of rambunctious kids—everyone's out hunting for treasure. The lust for submarine loot rolls in each time a strong sou'easter blows the water out. The phenomenon is rare, but when it happens, the wind picks up the river in its muscular hand and shoves the water tens of yards from shore. And much that was hidden lies open to the sky—natural detritus, like shells and sodden driftwood, mingled with centuries of plain old trash. This evening it's the trash that fascinates.

Within an hour the tornado watch has ended, though the wind still blows at half-gale strength. The river-walkers start to bring in their finds. Buckets are laden, and pockets and arms. The trophies soon cover the top of our outdoor table: bottles, bottles, and more bottles—tiny flagons that may once have held perfume; slightly larger ones bearing the impressed names of patent medicines; soda bottles of every hue, one with a date in the '40s. They're filled now with sand, algae, and wiggling creatures just big enough to be discerned by the human eye. It may not be odd that only Dorothy has come in with glass that's truly historic, though it has no economic value—the shards of handblown rum and gin bottles from the Revolutionary era. Like young 'uns who prefer a whole cookie to bits and pieces, most of tonight's adolescent scavengers are scanting elderly fragments in favor of cast-offs that have survived a mere few decades but are entire.

K.D. comes racing in. She, too, has bottles, clutching them between her sides and upper arms. Her hands hold something else. She thrusts it at me. Bottles drop to the ground but fortunately do not smash.

"What *is* it?" she says.

It's an oyster box, an empty shell with its two halves still attached at the hinge.

"I know that. Hold out your hands. What's *this*?"

173

She tips the oyster box over my cupped palms. "Don't lose it!" she cries.

All at once, I'm holding a fish. And the fish, a very small creature, returns my startled gaze and rolls its eyes with a why-me expression. We rush inside and put it in a bowl of tap water, where it swims vigorously. I haul out the reference books. Though I've never seen its like in the river before, this fish looks somehow familiar.

About three inches long. A thorough peppering of brown freckles over the lighter brown of its head, snout, and gill coverings. Irregular, greyish horizontal lines on its scaleless and elongate body. Pectoral fins like fans flipped open. A continuous dorsal fin rippling like a valance from just beyond the fish's nape all the way to its tail. And at the fin's anterior end, a spot as brightly turquoise-blue as a sea robin's eyes, as round as the never-sleeping eyes that are vigilant to see the way ahead for Achilles' beaked ship. The fish is a striped blenny, a male in breeding colors. Its species is one of seventeen New-World representatives of a large family known to the Greeks, whose generic word *blennos* has been applied by latter-day nomenclators to the whole kit and caboodle of the Blenniidae. K.D. may have interrupted this particular blenny at his amorous pursuits; his and several other blenny species have claimed clean oyster boxes as the spawning grounds of choice. And I learn why he looks like something I've met before: blennies swim in the show-room aquaria of dealers in tropical fish. His name and habits ascertained, he is returned forthwith to his own vital, salty affairs.

174

The blenny tumbles swift into my hand. Achilles' name does not present itself with such great speed but follows slowly on the apparition of the little fish. And when the name does come, weeks later, I am content and believe that it might satisfy both thwarted emperor and the blameless but pushy Sir Thomas.

Achilles and the blenny have something in common. At first, it seems to be that they hid themselves, the fish in a pearly shell, the boy not quite a man in secluded rooms that may have been decorated with bright murals of dancers, bulls, or dolphins. Creatures of all kinds conceal themselves: the red-brown Carolina wren deep in the red-brown pine-straw tunnel of her nest; the anole lizard matching its colors to its surroundings, grey-brown for bark, fresh green for honeysuckle leaves; the cottontail hiding in stillness; the pupa lying secret in a chrysalis made from its own skin. Simply by hiding himself, by letting himself be hidden, Achilles seems kin to them all. Then, I think that the fact of concealment makes for only a superficial likeness, the resemblance in a single aspect of one strawberry blond to every other. It isn't enough, not nearly enough, to establish his name. Slowly, slowly, it occurs to me to wonder, Why do they hide? I don't remember the instant of that question. I may have been fishing the net or putting supper on the stove or scratching a chigger bite. No matter. The name comes almost on the asking.

Sir Thomas, a rational man, says, "There is nothing strictly immortal, but immortality." Only the abstract idea can endure (though the Sirens would have us believe otherwise). None of us, despite our wishes and

175

our most fervid, state-of-the-art attempts, can ever save our mortal remains from dissolution. No funerary preparations of the most elaborate kinds, no means of disposal can ever save a whit of our physical substance. And scribble our names as we will on monuments, our memorial stones and pyramids and obelisks all crumble. Nor, though we earn resounding fame or notoriety, can we count on the memories of succeeding generations to preserve the never-tangible scraps of our existences—our deeds and names. Sir Thomas counsels that we not engage in any such hopeless scrabbles for some small immunity to our temporal condition but rather turn our efforts to the practice of an earthly humility that will gain us heaven.

In the daylit hours of every season—chilly, warm, hellacious hot—I roam our shore with Sally to see how birds and beasts conduct their lives. On winter nights, we huddle comfortably indoors with books, small talk, and scratches behind her velvet ears for Sal. But on other nights, we're outside answering the river's summons to set the gill net, keep watch for owls, or merely laze in the yard listening to the water beneath the shining legends. No constellation bears the name Achilles, nor would a man of such restless temper have wanted to join Cassiopeia and Pegasus and be immortalized as a radiant but forever frozen congeries of stars. Stars are for navigation, anyhow, for keeping the ships straight on their singing-and-dancing, dolphin-led course toward Troy.

Immortality is the antithesis of what most deeply concerns both blenny and nascent hero. Hiding was

important to Achilles after all, as important as it is to
fish and lizard, wren, rabbit, and butterfly-to-be. Once
his mother issued her orders, he had no choice but to
heed them; a deathless goddess brooks no disobedience
from a mortal son. I'm sure he was scared on arrival.
Nor was it the change in environment, the trading of
Kheiron's friendly squalor for prattle and politesse, that
frightened him. Terror thudded against his ribs and
greased his palms with sweat because he was given
sudden access to an unaccustomed state of being. He
was unbalanced not by physical imprisonment of his
body but by his spirit's need to find a new way of
looking at the world. Seeking equilibrium, Achilles
curled into himself, quiescent as a pupa that wiggles
only when it's touched.

I think that this is what happened. As misery bent
him unspeaking over the loom to which he'd been as-
signed, he stalked his boisterous, carefree boyhood
through memory's thickets, recalling the boar he'd
killed when he was six years old. The shouting pride of
that moment, his own and Kheiron's, echoed in the
cave of his longing—the tusker had been young but
big. Kheiron had demanded every detail of the hunt
and the kill. And so it had been each time Achilles
brought home the carcass of his prey: the telling was
both celebration and ritual prayer. But after each telling, Kheiron would turn from praise to gruff instruction, giving the same lesson so often that it was little
heeded. Now, bent to the wretched loom, Achilles listened.

I also listen. I eavesdrop from my distant vantage

point and even now hear Kheiron tutoring his unripe foster-son. Kheiron the centaur knows what he's talking about; half-man, half-stallion, he's always been privy to the wisdom of every animal, not just the human sort. He whickers and snorts, tail-whisks a fly from his left haunch, and strikes one hoof on the cave floor to gavel Achilles to attention. "Now whoa back, cub, you make it too hard on yourself. When you hunt, forget about thinking. Just *be*. Be that lion or stag you got your mind set on." Sternly, he tells his pupil, "Damn it, you little cur, use the good animal sense you was born with."

The centaur's language is casual, earthy, but the import of his words is one with which modern investigators of perception would agree. Translated into their terms, Kheiron's lesson tries to pound into Achilles the idea that humankind operates under two systems of perception, ordinary and simultaneous. *Homo sapiens* usually settles for the armchair comfort of the ordinary mode, in which each one of us is a separate entity observing, and differentiating self from, the other people, things, and happenings in our environs but not acting until something lands a swift kick in the seat of self-interest. Ordinary perception looks inward: how do my surroundings affect *me*? It is a mode within which people often function well indeed; it also causes names to be neatly engraved on tombstones, gouged crudely into trees, or scratched on walls. Simultaneous perception looks outward. The barriers between self and everything else dissolve. (Sir Thomas might have considered this condition a good move toward humil-

ity and, eventually, heaven. Kheiron calls it *kairos*—
balance. And as I listen in, I realize that the Sirens'
trick is to promise simultaneity—awareness of everything at once—but the call is lethally false.) When barriers melt, all five senses attend equally and without
particular emphasis to everything the occasion and the
place present. We become linked to and involved with
all that surrounds us. Purposiveness ceases to be the
private fief of the individual, for everything is understood to be invested with its own reason for existence.
And we who are human become otters, wrens, fish, or
centaurs, alert as always to self but also registering
every signal the environment sends—the angle of sun,
the plash of water, the hidden or bumptious there-ness
of other life. How marvelous, to move easily among a
thousand sensory impressions without bumping headlong into any one of them! How restful, to know in a
gut-way that we can respond—boom!—to a signal that
starts to whoop and holler.

I stand with my ear pressed close to the past.
Kheiron admonishes Achilles: "Stay separate, you're a
signal loud as a battlecry. Merge, the animals won't
know you're there, they'll walk right up, nibble your
hand or, more likely, mark your leg with a good squirt
of piss. Cub, you hear one word I said?"

At the loom, Achilles finally heard and understood.
He shed his separateness like a too-small skin. And
right there in plain sight, he hid. There in the women's
quarters, he merged so completely into his surroundings that he vanished to everyone but himself. Plying
the shuttle, he hunkered down into the animal part of

179

himself and existed, like other creatures, in the present, not brooding on past or future but giving whole allegiance to all that was immediate. Amid the myriad signals broadcast by his closed-in universe, he rested easy, sure that he could rise to action if necessary—quell the most earsplitting arguments or make love during siestas lauded by snores and soft-rustling sheets. (Good girl who mothered his son—she didn't tattle.)

For blenny in his clean box, for wren in her nest and lizard among the leaves, hiding is a basic strategy that fosters attainment of a fundamental goal: not individual survival but continuation of their kind. For Achilles, not yet metamorphosed into warrior, hiding gave instruction in the art of gaining equipoise, of becoming one with the world into which he had been thrust with peremptory speed. But more than that, hiding forced him to the core of his being, a core inescapably shared with every swimming, leaping, flying thing.

An older voice rumbles basso into the chorus of Greeks, Tiberius, and Sir Thomas—the Hebraic voice of *Deuteronomy:* "I call heaven and earth to record this day against you, that I have set before you life and death, blessing and cursing: therefore choose life, that both thou and thy seed may live."

"All right, my young bawling sea-calf, choose your own name," Thetis had said just before she bundled her robe-swaddled son off to the boondocks. Achilles had reached deep into the grab-bag of his rage, clutched at a word that Kheiron often used in speaking of animals, and spat it at her. It was never a throwaway alias, though he tucked it out of mind when he slid back into ordinariness and reached for that glittering armor. Nor was it an attempt at finding singularity. It was an acknowledgment. A good, old Greek name, one that even now finds currency though modern fashion has decreed it out of style, it states the rock-bottom business of fish and hero and dolphin, of Sally, the Chief and me, of every breathing mortal thing. Achilles' luck, the luck of all who are human, is that we can recognize and humbly seize the present moment, if only we will. Achilles' name? Zoë, of course. Life.